Special Message
From The Author

This book is a recollection of my experiences while attending Florida State University High School in Tallahassee, Florida from 1964 to 1968. Also included are experiences that directly impacted my maturation during that period. These events are true and only a few names were changed. There are a few occasions in the book, however, where conversations and scenarios between individuals outside my presence were chronicled. Such conversations and scenarios were obviously products of my imagination, albeit an imagination inclusive of knowledge of the involved characters, the contextual circumstances of the conversation, and a consideration of relevant preceding or subsequent supportive facts.

Please note that the "N-word" is utilized with some frequency in this book. While I am (and always have been) incredibly offended by its use by Whites towards Blacks, I recognize that this degrading word has no place when used within the Black community. The historical context of the word's usage emphasizes that its utilization by Whites towards Blacks has had an intended degrading purpose that comes from an ugly past when it was used to describe Black ancestry as chattel, later as sub-human, and post-Civil War as second-class citizens. In my experience especially the period of my life covered in this book when I was labeled the N-word to my face by White bigots, there was no question they did so for one purpose- and that was to make me feel like my race alone made me less than them regardless of objective evidence quite to the contrary.

This book was written with no malice whatsoever toward any referenced characters. I hope that in its totality including use of the N-word will provide my readers an accurate description of some of the struggles and challenges which integrationist pioneers were confronted with during their own periods of maturation when trying to effect social change in a country where the majority has sought to continue the oppressive status quo.

Evolution Of An Integrationist

My Navigation Through
Race Relations & Maturation
1964-1968

Keith W. Neyland, J.D.

Evolution Of An Integrationist: My Navigation Through Race
Relations & Maturation.

Written: Keith W. Neyland
Edited: Keith W. Neyland, Lindsey Neyland & Trish Geran
Cover Design/Typography Layout: Trish Geran

Neyland, Keith W.
Autobiography
  1. Neyland, Keith W., 1950-
  2. Race relations at Florida State University High School from 1964-1968.
  3. The struggles and challenges of an integration pioneer.

CONTENTS

Special Message From the Author

Acknowledgments

ACKNOWLEDGEMENTS

I want to acknowledge the highly supportive people in my life whose invaluable assistance has facilitated my completion of this book written bit by bit over a thirty-year span. The priority by which I identify those who provided me assistance on this project does not necessarily reflect the degree to which their support impacted its completion. I honestly can't quantify such, nor do I feel any need to do so. Suffice to say that without my support group, it may have taken another thirty years for me to complete this book.

In any event, I want to thank my daughter Lindsey Wallis Neyland for her on-going assessments (and related compliments or criticisms) of various portions of this project as she typed each into book-form. Former English major that she was, she kept me positive by advising me when she thought I'd done something well and she kept me humble when she criticized. Always a fair critic of my communicative skills, it was comforting when potions of the book were deemed by her to be okay.

As depicted in my book, my dad, Dr. Leedell W. Neyland was my impetus to begin my integration experience. He was always a high profile presence at FHS throughout my four years there-coming to athletic practices and games (even many away games where he'd more than likely be the only African American in the stadium or gym other than me) and all PTA meetings. I found it eminently reassuring that he visited FHS so much to look out for me even though he'd had a few racial slurs directed at him there. I never questioned whether he had my back. He has served as a lighthouse in all aspects of my life and has guided me through many storms and much murky water.

I want to graciously acknowledge my late Mother, Della Louise Neyland, from whom my sense of empathy is derived. Growing up, I recognized my mom's incredible kindness and nearly universal love of people. My emulation of my mom in this regard facilitated my acceptance of many of the lessons I learned during the four years that are the subject of this book. Another positive I derived from my mom (and my dad) was that no matter the circumstances, I was never to allow my dignity to be compromised.

As reflected in this book, my sister, Dr. Beverly Ann Neyland, has always exemplified drive and positive ambition. She's always been strong as a rock and she has been for me, and many others, an incredibly positive role model. I've tried to emulate her drive through the years especially her tenacity in attaining goals she's set for herself. I've also tried to emulate one of her other inherent attributes---a classy persona exhibited by her quiet dignity, self-confidence and self-respect.

I'd like to acknowledge my younger sister, Katrina D. Brown. Since birth, she has lived with a profound physical challenge which has robbed her of her ability to walk. Even with such a challenge, Karina has finished college, earned a Master's Degree, and worked at the FAMU School of Pharmacy where she was once voted Faculty Counselor of the Year. Katina's many successes in the context of her disability have truly inspired me and taught me that there are no excuses for failing to diligently pursue one's goals no matter the challenges of life confronted.

I want to acknowledge Marion my lovely wife's, contribution to completion of this book. She has been steadfastly supportive on a day-to-day basis like, for example, those occasions that she acquiesced to my getting up to write on "my story" at 4:00 a.m. even though my doing so awoke her for the morning. She helped me immensely by coordinating my scheduled health treatments and by, otherwise, helping to organize my available time to work on this project. She has been consistently encouraging that I work on the book when I felt the inclination to do so (and many times when I had no such inclination) though some such occasions disrupted her highly maintained order of things.

Lastly, I want acknowledge Trish Geran, my publicist for the invaluable assistance she has provided relative to preparation of this book for publication. Given my total ignorance of that process, Trish with requisite professionalism has walked me through the necessary requirements on a comprehensive basis to fully turn the draft of a story into publishable book form.

Deal with yourself as an individual worthy of respect
and make everyone else deal with you the same way.
---Nikki Giovanni.

If you have no confidence in self, you are twice
defeated in the race of life. With confidence, you
have won even before you have started.
---Marcus Garvey

Life is not about waiting for the storms to pass.
It's about learning to dance in the rain.
---Anonymous

1964-65
FRESHMAN

To be honest, I don't remember exactly when or how my dad brought up the prospect of my integrating an all-White school in my hometown of Tallahassee in 1964. But sometime in early summer of that year, I agreed to leave my comfortable learning environment in the small school district associated with Florida A&M University, the all-Black college where my dad worked as the Dean of Arts and Science, to matriculate as a rising freshman at Florida High School in the school district associated with Florida State University, racially the stark mirror image of FAMU. I don't recall giving that decision a lot of thought; rather, I was content to rely on my dad's judgment as to what was best for me. If Dr. Leedell Neyland thought my integrating a school would provide a more beneficial academic environment than staying at the Black school where coincidently my older sister, Beverly, had thrived, I was convinced that I would and, indeed, should make that move. I made the decision to agree to the transfer and thereafter did not question its appropriateness.

So starting in the early summer of 1964, my dad had several visits with Mr. Clay Bishop, the principal and other administrators at Florida High School. In late July, my dad returned home from one such meeting and advised me that he and the Florida High administrators had agreed that it would be best if I had a Black companion so that I was not endeavoring to integrate Florida High by myself. Called upon to pick a fellow student to join me at Florida High, I immediately thought of my friend Mahlon Rhaney, a classmate of mine with whom I regularly competed for the highest grades since I first began attending the elementary school on FAMU's campus in the fourth grade. While Mahlon and I had never

12

been the closest of friends, we were close enough with both of us having a strong interest in sports.

Mahlon and his family were not hesitant in agreeing to have him join me as one of Florida High's first two Black students. We were immediately advised by Principal Bishop that we should not consider playing football or basketball because there existed too great a potential for the infliction of "outside-of-the-rules" injuries. He suggested that if we wanted to participate in sports, we limit such participation to track. I guess he assumed we were fast runners.

Neither Mahlon nor I was thrilled about the prohibition against laying basketball, a sport we loved but had never played on an organized basis. We knew, however, that we'd encounter enough challenges just being students in school day to day. Neither of us had ever interacted with White folks before. Living on or around the campus of Florida A&M University we rarely encountered White people except on weekly trips with our mothers to the Winn-Dixie grocery store, Sears and Roebuck, or less frequently, downtown stores. In those passing encounters, White people would pass us in the aisles as if they did not see us, and we would pass them in the same manner.

Compounding my isolation from White society, I remember that, at that time, there were virtually no Black people on TV, except Amos 'N Andy. Black music was rarely heard on Tallahassee's radio stations, and even the sports teams viewable on weekends largely consisted of all-White SEC teams and, on Sundays, the regularly-featured all-White Washington Redskins.

Except for the all-Black Leon Theater, which featured Mantan Molan and other "Colored movies," there were no movie houses from which people of color were not strictly barred. Until the Howard Johnson Motel restaurant opened up, no Tallahassee restaurants would serve us. Consequently, on those Sundays that he took his family out to eat, my dad would drive us the 20 miles to the little town of St. Mark's on the Gulf, to a small Black restaurant-rundown though it was-where we got the best fried seafood combination plates imaginable. Clearly, our integration of Florida High was going to place me and Mahlon directly in an alien world, a world populated by people who we believed were so different from us. A people about whom we knew very little except that, based on our limited experiences, they despised us.

13

However, after my first actual visit to Florida High, I thought I had gotten it all wrong. They did not seem to despise us at all. Per written invitation from the school's Key Club, Mahlon and I attended a "welcoming orientation" a couple of days before school formally started. Nervous in our first real visit to Florida High, we were pleasantly surprised to find that many of the dozen or so of the coat-and-tied young men who comprised our welcoming committee were quite friendly, extending welcomes that seemed heartfelt. Some, though smiling, seemed noticeably uncomfortable talking to Mahlon and me. I did not hear the word Nigger once. One of the Key Club members, in a sincere effort to make conversation, asked if I knew Lucinda Williams who had worked for his family for almost twenty years. I postured like I was thinking long and hard before telling him that her name did not ring a bell. It was clear that the orientation had been just for Mahlon and me; no other new students were there. Going home that night, I realized that the sense of dread that I had felt upon learning that Mahlon and I were to be integration pioneers had significantly dissipated. Notwithstanding the hostilities that Whites were generally directing at Black folks uppity enough to rock the boat of racial status quo, the White students at Florida High were obviously different-a more accepting, tolerant group too sophisticated to hate us solely because of the color of our skin. I slept better that night than I had in weeks, this integration stuff would not be so bad at Florida High.

I was wrong. Any hopes that we had had on arriving the first day of school that we would see similarly friendly, smiling faces like those displayed by the Key Club members at our earlier personal orientation were quickly dispelled. As we walked down the long hallways, groups of students would stop on-going, conversations and stare as we walked by. Some of the students in the various groups remained quiet as we passed, and because we pointedly avoided looking at them, it was not clear what their sentiments were-racial hatred, indifferent curiosity, shock, or some combination. Some big, football types dramatically pointed at us, while laughing and elbowing one another. "I can't believe we got Niggers here now," someone shouted.

For some reason I looked over in that direction. A big guy with a huge neck and a crew-cut, his face instantly squinting up into a hateful mask, yelled in a surprisingly high voice, "What you looking at

14

Nigger?" I looked away as we continued to walk and realized that was the first time a White person had called me Nigger to my face. However, that novelty quickly wore off since it happened several times before I reached where my first class at Florida High was scheduled to be held-in Room 201.

Apparently to break the monotony of mere name-calling, one boy dramatically plastered his back against a wall, arms outspread, as if he were trying to avoid any possibility of coming in contact with us. Another student started making sounds like a gorilla as we passed. The group around him laughed elbowing one another at his exhibition.

Mahlon's first class was Spanish and it was in Room 211. Before I turned into 201, I watched a moment as he continued down the hall. As pitiful as we must have looked walking the hostile hallways together, I could tell by the slump in Mahlon's shoulders that it was even worse walking them alone. And, as he walked away from me down the hall, he could not have looked more alone.

Of course, he was no more alone than I found myself when I entered Room 201. The buzz of conversation among the students who half-filled Mr. Holroyd's freshman English class ended abruptly when my presence was noticed and the ensuing silence seemed louder. A boy in the back row jumped up as I proceeded to the nearly empty front row. I heard him yell at the doorway, "Hey Mike, I got a Nigger in my class." I sat down with empty desks flanking my right and left. I realized that of all things, I was embarrassed. The boy's ignorance in loudly labeling me did not make me angry or scare me. What I felt instead was the same thing I'd felt during the earlier displays of degradation-humiliation, undoubtedly what I was supposed to feel.

As the class slowly filled up, the seats on opposite sides of me remained empty. Someone in the back started throwing spitballs at me. I looked back after the first one flew over my head. A big guy in a t-shirt hatefully stared defiantly into my eyes. Then something totally unexpected happened. A boy, sitting on the end of the second row, got up and took a few steps in my direction. He was a little bigger than me and I momentarily braced myself for some sort of attack. Instead, he sat down at the desk next to mine and leaned his head towards me, "Hi. My name is Tim Garland." A spitball smacked against my back as I told Tim my name. Then Mr. Holroyd, bespectacled, short and thin, walked in. The first thing he did was point to the handful of spitballs around my desk.

"Who's responsible for this?" he said while pointing at the area around my desk. He looked in the back row of seats where three guys who looked too old to be freshmen sat with their heads down. "Anything else like this kind of stuff will get people sent to the principal's office, I mean it." After a lengthy silence during which he pointedly looked at the three boys in the back row, he introduced himself and began teaching the class.

My heart started racing the closer it came to the end of class. I knew that I would soon be leaving the relative safety of the classroom to again face the almost certain humiliation and possible aggression my schoolmates would direct toward me during the ebb and flow of the between-class migrations. My next class, French, was down the hall. As students were going up and down the hallway, I encountered more of what Mahlon and I'd gotten earlier, except the name-calling varied to include "Coon," an epithet I had never heard before. As I walked down the hall trying simultaneously to ignore the indignities and to keep a lookout for possible acts of violence, I saw three approaching upperclassmen looking at me in a furtive way while leaning their heads close together conspiratorially. I knew they were up to something and that, whatever it was, I probably wouldn't like it.

As I moved closer to the left wall of the hall, the three of them walking shoulder to shoulder veered ever so slightly towards me. Just as I was about to pass them, the one closest to me bumped into me with his shoulder and knocked me against the wall. They laughed, so proud of themselves, and kept walking. I noticed other students laughing and felt the all too familiar flush of humiliation. But I felt something else: something that came from a deeper place than had the humiliation. I felt an almost primal surge of anger. I righted myself and kept walking. I was most angry because my failure to fight back made me look and feel like a coward. I could not help thinking about the truism that I had tried to ingrain in my psyche upon learning I was coming to Florida High: simply, that calling me a Nigger did not make me one. I could not escape feeling, however, that if I permitted myself to be physically bullied, I would be a coward whether I was called that or not.

As I continued to walk, I ignored the on-going stupidity directed at me by the students. I wondered whether the White kids felt that as a Black person I was more likely to meekly accept bullying. I found myself concluding that though I could never stop the name-calling, I could control whether I was going to be a coward. I told myself that I would have to fight back when physically attacked. As I tried to buoy my confidence that I would thereafter take on any of my physical tormenters, I had some harsh realities to confront.

I was skinny as a rail and frankly not the toughest guy around; and the idea of beating up White people was something that was, in that place and time, pretty much unheard of for folks of color except, God knows, in professional boxing rings. I told myself as I approached my next classroom that I nevertheless had to stand up for my newly-formulated convictions. Not just for me; I could not stop thinking that I had to show some courage for other Black people-folks who, for the first time, I realized I represented whether I wanted to or not.

After French, I hooked up with Mahlon; we shared the same schedule after second period. It was amazing to me how much more comfortable I was walking through the stares, epithets and other hateful displays with Mahlon instead of alone. I told him, "Man, a couple of these 'Crackers' bumped me against a wall."

Shaking his head and his black eyes looking directly at me, he said, "I know what you talking about. One went by me and threw a pencil." "What did you do?" I asked him. He waited a moment and responded defensively, "Other than duck, nothing. What did you do?" "I didn't do anything either but kept walking," I replied. "Keith, we got to stand up against the physical shit, man, or they gonna start slapping us around for fun." "You're right my Brother. You're right. That's exactly how I feel."

We walked on in silence as the drama of name-calling, pointing and gorilla imitations continued to surround us. Two skinny Black ninth-graders-alone as two humans could be in a crowd of other humans-had agreed on a "fight back" theory; its execution, we both knew, could prove painfully problematic, particularly since in the past several years the only people Mahlon and I had fought had been two bouts with each other. Neither altercation had been much of a fight, and we each had won one. I looked at the size of some of the upper-class guys going up and down the halls and tried to envision fighting them. It was not a pleasant thought.

Mahlon had obviously been having his own personal reality check. "Man, we could be wearing ass-kickings every day."

Within the hour, we gratefully learned that our wardrobes would probably not include daily ass-kickings. During third period, we went to the auditorium for a scheduled school-wide assembly. Sitting in an island of empty seats, Mahlon and I could not block out the fact that, even in that mass of students, the two of us were still the centers of attention. Some students stood up in their seats to get better looks at the two Black novelties amid much finger-pointing. Mahlon and I were infamous celebrities immediately identifiable no matter where we were at dear old Florida High.

I found myself missing how I blended in at my old homogeneous school. There, it was my choice whether I wanted to standout-through loud, obnoxious behavior or any other conduct that would make my schoolmates notice me. At Florida High, my presence was enough, nothing more was needed. I sat there next to Mahlon in silence feeling overwhelmed-doubting, for the first time that day, whether I would make it in the integration business.

As more students filed in, Tim came over and sat next to me with two friends of his sitting next to him. He introduced the crew-cut boy sitting immediately next to him as Stan Dietrich. I, in turn, introduced Mahlon to Tim and Stan. More heads turned to look our way and there seemed to be a louder buzz in the auditorium. I distinctly heard a boy's voice from a couple of rows behind us: "Look at those Nigger-lovers." I glanced over at Tim. He had to have heard it but he did not look back. I noticed his face began to redden. It occurred to me that with my dark complexion, and my physiological inability to turn red, my inner feelings were that much harder to read. I knew that for me at Florida High, that was a good thing.

The President of the Student Union gave a welcoming speech, which was followed by Principal Bishop. He spoke about how good he expected the school year to be and the positive tradition Florida High had in academics, sports, and the high character of its students and graduates. He then segued into a general welcome to all new students, paused, and went on to say:

"I want to offer a special welcome to our two new students who transferred here from Florida A&M University junior high-Keith Neyland and Mahlon Rhaney. I want you to know that we are proud to have you join us here at Florida High. I want it to be extra clear to everybody here that any mistreatment of these two students, or indeed, of any students, will be severely dealt with. But make no mistake, if there occur any assaults of our new students on the basis of their race, the involved students will face expulsion. Just remember, we're not a public school. We're a demonstration school for FSU, a teaching school if you will. Nobody has a right to be here and serious misconduct will result in immediate suspension and expulsion."

Hearing the Principal say these words was uplifting. It sure looked like he had our backs and we were not totally alone. I felt encouraged knowing I would not be involved in daily fights to defend myself and my race.

After the assembly, we headed to the cafeteria. While standing in line, we quickly saw that the light of our celebrity had hardly dimmed. It seemed like everyone continued to stare at us. Immediately in front of us were a couple of upper-class students-a boy and a girl. Before he realized that we were standing behind him, the boy had his arm tightly around the girl's shoulder. After noticing us, he kept turning and looking disgustedly at us and started talking animatedly with the girl.

"Look at them," he nodded his head back at us. "I ain't standing here next to no Niggers. Let's go." He took a couple of steps out of line turning as he did toward the back of the cafeteria. The girl did not move. He stepped back in her direction. "Sherrie, come on. We ain't gonna stand here next to them Coons." He leaned in closer. "You ain't no Nigger-lover are you?" He turned and began walking toward the back of the line.

The girl stood there a moment. She had to know that since so many students were looking at Mahlon and me, they all had to be viewing her drama. She turned and started after her boyfriend. In passing by us, she looked into my eyes and mouthed, "I'm sorry."

Mahlon leaned over towards me. "We haven't been here but half a day, and already, two good-looking soul brothers got White boys running scared and White women acting all confused because of our good looks." We had one of the few real laughs we'd had all day. I thought, let them wonder about what we could possibly have to laugh at.

A couple of the cafeteria ladies smiled at us warmly as they put a cheeseburger and fries on our plates. With trays also laden with a little bowl of salad, a serving of banana pudding, and two mini-milk cartons, we headed out to get our seats. All the tables were occupied to one degree or another in the small eating area. We sat at a table with two empty seats on the end. Immediately the students closest to us got up and left the table dispersing to sit anywhere other than with us. We had the table to ourselves except for two students at the far end who did not move, and, for that matter, did not look up. We sat there and ate hungrily-Mahlon systematically taking small bites and me nervously, almost maniacally, gulping my food down. The meal, while objectively hot and delicious, was almost tasteless with the dozens of eyes focused, at least it seemed, on our every chew.

A few minutes after we sat down, I waited over an empty plate as Mahlon finished his lunch. Two upper-class boys who welcomed us during the Key Club orientation, walked over to our table. One of them smiled broadly, the other's smile seemed uncomfortably forced as his eyes seem to keep looking around as if to see who was looking.

The big-smiler who leaned over to me and placed his hands on the back of an empty chair said, "I know it's been tough on y'all and it's going to be tough for a long time. I don't know if y'all remember me from the orientation the other night, but my name is Driggs-Jack Driggs." Nodding toward the other guy, Driggs continued, "This is Joe Cramer." Joe gave us a self-conscious half wave. Jack looked at Mahlon and then at me. "I just want you boys to know that everybody is not against you, although it might seem that way. Y'all just got to hang in there. There's a lot of decent kids here. Some of them, probably most of them, may not like this integration thing, but they won't stoop to the ignorant name-calling and that other racial crap. But like y'all have seen, there are sho'enough who will. Y'all just got to be strong."

Without waiting for a response, they both turned and walked

away. Mahlon looked over at me. "That was nice. They didn't have to do that especially in here in front of all the junior Kluxxers."

I said, "Isn't that the truth." Then, I noticed one face seemed to jump into focus at a table to our left because of the palpable hatred it reflected. It was the kind of hatred that no one could fake, and because of its intensity, I almost could not turn away. I recognized him as one of the guys who had thrown spitballs at me during English. When our eyes locked, he slowly, dramatically, raised a middle finger in my direction and just held it there.

"Hey Bro," I said to Mahlon, "Check out the Cracker to your left."

As Mahlon turned to see what was going on, I allowed my focus to broaden and noticed that immediately around the boy making the provocative gesture were several other guys staring intently at us with hateful glares, although none was as disturbing as the one gesturing in our direction.

Standing up and picking up my tray, I said, "Let's get the hell out of here."

Mahlon who had already started to stand up, said "You know no matter what happens-how well we dress, how smart we are, anything, there's always going to be a bunch of them that will hate our guts."

As we walked out, it occurred to me that I had never had anybody really even dislike me before, at least that I was aware of; and now, in less than four hours, without my having changed at all, I had a bunch of people who seriously hated me.

The rest of the school day was a mirror image of its first half with one exception. Our fifth period Phys. Ed class was uniquely memorable. After reporting to the boys' locker room, we met Coach Dick Rose, the Head Football Coach and our Physical Education teacher. He had us line up in two rows. Coach Rose was deeply tanned and spoke with a rich, molasses drawl. His blue eyes were piercing and as they bore into each of our faces; they seemed in search of each of our candy-ass quotient. I recalled that was the way Coach Bobby Lang would look at you back at FAMU Junior High. That way of looking at you, I concluded, must have been a coach's way of determining how long the journey would be to turn you from a boy to a man using whatever standards high school coaches use in making that call.

After giving us our locker numbers and lock combinations, he said, "Men, I got certain expectations. I expect y'all to be on time and to be in your gym stuff by 2:08. That's not 2:10, Hurley." He smiled broadly at a muscular guy who I later found out was a good, up-and-coming JV football player.

"All of y'all will participate in the sports activity scheduled. Don't bother bringing in notes from your momma saying that "Little Junior" has a cold and can't do this or that. The only reason I will allow any of y'all to miss a scheduled P.E. activity is if you're having yo' monthly period. Now that won't be an issue with any of you young men, will it?"

Only Hurley answered," No sir, Coach."

Coach Rose looked at us in disgust. "Is Hurley the only one that won't have monthly female problems? Is that gonna be an issue for any of the rest of you?"

Mahlon and I joined in the collective, "No sir, Coach." "Alright, that's good to know." He walked over to where Mahlon and I stood. He smiled at Mahlon. "And which one are you?" Looking momentarily confused, Mahlon hesitated, "I'm Mahlon Rhaney."

Coach Rose turned his attention to me. "That means you must be Keith."

I said, "Yes, sir."

"Which one of you is the fastest?"

"I am," I said.

He brought his face closer to mine. "You fast as Bob Hayes?" he said with twinkling eye. (Hayes was the 100 yard dash collegiate champion at FAMU). "Not yet," I said.

He laughed as if that had been the funniest thing he'd ever heard. "Not yet," he repeated. "We'll see, 'cause we gonna play a little football today. Now, y'all hurry and get dressed in your gym stuff and be out at the field in five minutes."

As we changed into our gym shorts and shirts, I noticed that our environment was not nearly as racially charged as the classrooms, lunchroom and hallways had been earlier. Indeed, one boy whose locker happened to be between mine and Mahlon's introduced himself to both of us as Larry LaSeur. Notably, however, he dressed quickly and left. When I took off my pants to put on my gym shorts, I was confronted with an ugly truth. "Hey Sticks," using the nickname which best described his legs. "Man I've had a visit from the Ash Fairy."

Mahlon looked over at my gray, scaly legs. "Damn, man. Please tell me you didn't forget your Jergens."

"I did," I admitted. "You wouldn't have happened to have brought any did you?"

"No," he answered. "Lotion was not one of the things I thought about today, man."

I looked over at Mahlon with his tawny complexion. He did not have the acute need for Jergens that I clearly did. As I closed my locker and we headed towards the field, I whispered in his ear, "You know I may never bring any Jergens over here, 'cause gray as I get without it, I blend in with the White folk better." He shook his head. "No lie."

The ensuing touch football game was fun. At the beginning, under Coach Rose's close supervision, I was the first pick by Hurley, who along with another junior varsity football player, had been appointed captain, charged with selecting their team's members. Football was my favorite sport; I probably played more touch football with my neighborhood friends than any other sport and I was pretty good. I was fast and elusive enough to almost always make players miss me in the open field. I had a field day with my fellow ninth-graders, making them miss their efforts to apply the two-hand touch and scoring almost at will. I also played some quarterback and prided myself on my ability to pass accurately while running left or right. As we ran past Coach Rose to the lockers to get dressed, it seemed that his stare followed me as I ran, appraisingly. I smiled; it didn't seem to bother him that I'd forgotten my Jergens.

After getting dressed and as we walked down the hall past Coach Rose's office, his gruff voice called out, "Keith, come in here a minute."

I stopped, pivoted, and went into the office without saying a word to Mahlon.

Coach Rose stood up behind his desk. "You can run like a scared jackrabbit. I guess I have to admit it, y'all just tend to be faster, shiftier than we are." Not knowing what to say, I said nothing.

"Someday, it ain't out of the question, you could be wearing the maroon and white of our Demon football team. Especially the way things have been changing. I don't know, but someday I could see you catching long passes from my son, Ben, he's a sophomore and a quarterback. You could be the "Black Lightning" of our football team." He seemed to catch himself as if he'd been daydreaming out loud. "But like I said that's somewhere down the road, if it happens at all." He smiled, "Anyway, Lightning, I'll see you tomorrow."

I left and realized that I had not said a word in the office. When I stepped into the hallway, Mahlon was waiting. I knew he would be.

"Brother you showed off some Black Power in that PE class," he said. "You ran so fast, I thought either the Klan was after your ass or you had kissed a White girl in Mississippi."

Mahlon, whose best sport was baseball where he was a real good left-handed pitcher, continued the compliments and I ate them up. It made me feel good to think I was a better athlete than the White boys. Almost on cue, we passed two upperclassmen who looked like football players. One said "Hey you Black Nigger, I hear you think you're a hotshot ballplayer. Well that's just with those little ninth-graders. Anyway that's all you jungle bunnies can do is run fast and jump high. Y'all ain't got no heart. So don't think yo' Black ass is special."

Mahlon and I walked on in silence. I realized that in the past ten minutes I had been likened to a scared jack rabbit and called a jungle bunny. I no longer found myself feeling high about my athletic ability; a lot of White people obviously found my athleticism to be animalistic in nature-like I was less human than them. I knew that I would show those rednecks that I was as human if not more human than they were. I mean, after all, the guy had just said, "Y'all ain't got no heart." I could never imagine butchering grammar like that, given the impeccable English spoken in my house. As obviously low-class as that boy was, he thought he was superior to me. That had to be a joke. But somehow I knew it wasn't.

I know I had never been happier to see my family's green and white Dodge before when it pulled up in front of Florida High at the end of the school day. We hurried out; our first day as integration pioneers was officially over. I had an incredible sense of relief like a ton of pressure had been removed from my shoulders. It was so good to know that for the next 16 hours, I would not be called a Nigger by White people or otherwise denigrated. I kept telling myself

24

that I would never have another first day integrating dear old Florida High. The next day had to be easier, but I dreaded the sun's rising the next morning. The misery of the first day would be similarly replayed; it was unavoidable. Despite that, I never considered quitting.

We, of course, never had another first day at FHS and I thanked God for that small measure of grace. To be honest, as the first few days passed, we became more comfortable, at least becoming better oriented getting familiar with our schedules, teachers, and the students in our different classes. I noticed that for whatever reason, I had some early trouble distinguishing some of my classmates from others. Maybe it was because I had had so little experience ever interacting with White people before and had never really had a reason or the inclination to ever really focus on the details of their appearance. I found that I got better telling them apart, however, because it helped in identifying those that openly made our lives miserable. Part of our everyday stress involved our very real, though largely ineffective, efforts to avoid coming in contact with those students.

One student who refused to let me avoid him was the upperclassman who had purposely bumped into me on my first day. On the next two days, the same scenario played out. While walking with the same two boys, he would steer the other two while walking three abreast such that when I passed he could shoulder-shiver me knocking me off stride. The first two times, all three looked back and laughed.

On the third day, I noticed, only the guy who had bumped me looked back. I guessed the novelty had worn off for my tormentor's two buddies and my physical harassment had apparently become a mere routine. Despite all the name-calling and other verbal and non-verbal acts of degradation, my jousting during my walk down the hallway from English class to French class was the only physical provocation I encountered. It was apparent that that guy was the only one in the school willing to defy Principal Bishop's warning that we "soul brothers" were not to be touched.

On the third night, I found it hard to sleep. Thoughts of being pushed around in the hallway were getting difficult to shake. I knew I could identify the boy to the principal and the matter would be handled; but there was something distasteful to me about having to run to White folks to save me without making any effort to defend myself, especially since the boy (a senior) bumping me was not that much bigger than me. In my mind, I replayed my tough guy resolution of not being physically bullied, but it did not help me sleep any better that night.

Nevertheless, the next day, as I left English class, I felt like a young Nat Turner-determined to stand up and fight back. I wasn't sure how brave I'd really be under the circumstances, but I knew I was, or would be, too ashamed not to stand up for myself. I started repeating a saying I had seen somewhere before: "If you don't stand for something, you'll fall for anything." As fate would have it, Tim, for the first time, chose to walk with me to the French class we shared. We talked about our assignment (to name in French what we had eaten the night before and for breakfast that morning) I noticed the three upperclassmen inch closer to the path I was walking on.

As Tim rattled on, totally oblivious to what was about to occur, I switched my notebook and books to my left arm thereby freeing my right arm. My heart was racing, although their approach seemed to be playing out in slow motion. As they started to pass, the boy who always bumped into me made his move to push his shoulder into me as he had repeatedly done before. Only this time, just before he actually touched me, I forcefully swung my elbow into his shoulder. Given my previous passivity, he had no reason to have expected me to retaliate in kind. With his books flying out of his hands, he fell back onto his friends who caught him inches before he hit the floor. His beet-red face registered both surprise and embarrassment.

His friends helped to stand him up, and he tried to regroup. "Watch it Nig," he said, half-heartedly.

I kept an eye on him in case he wanted to come at me, but he quickly bent over to pick up his books, turned around, and with his two buddies walked away. None of them was laughing and since a number of students had witnessed the scene I had to believe the three of them may have been feeling some of the humiliation I felt every day.

Tim and I continued walking to French class. "I guess French toast would be toast de'francais," he said as if the mini-drama had not just played out in front of his eyes.

"That sounds about right to me," I responded.

For a change, I was walking away from a racial encounter

with my head high. I found that I was glad that Tim had seen me stand up for myself. After all, he had put himself on the line to befriend me. The least I could do was show him, as well as myself, that I had some self-respect and would not willingly accept victim status. For the record, the guy never bumped into me again and for that matter, noticeably avoided making even eye contact with me the rest of the year.

After resolving that adversarial situation, there were still plenty of day-to-day stressful occurrences to make us acutely aware that some form of humiliation could be waiting around each and every turn. The most guaranteed stress we encountered each day was at lunchtime. During lunch, whenever Mahlon and I entered the relatively small cafeteria, it seemed as though talking and eating would freeze at many of the tables as students stared at us. With the potential emptying of any table at which we sat, and the omnipresent stares as we ate, we eventually viewed lunchtime as easily the most emotionally trying segment of the day. We, nevertheless, dug deep and suffered through the forty-five minute ordeal. We found that if we hustled to lunch so that we arrived before the masses, we could find an empty table thereby removing the painful sight of students scurrying to other tables as if we were lepers.

After a couple of weeks, we had clearly become less of a novelty and, to be sure, except for a couple of pockets of die-hard racists, we were not stared at during lunchtime as we had been in the earlier days. But the lunch experience was still unpleasant enough that we just decided one day when we had arrived at the cafeteria later than normal that we were not up to the table-clearing scenario. We decided just to pass up lunch altogether. Knowing that there were few places on campus where we could hang during lunchtime without drawing undue attention, we decided to pass our lunch period behind the gymnasium. The relief we felt in avoiding the certain discomfort we knew we would endure in the cafeteria was almost negated by the intense hunger pains we faced later that day. We agreed to skip lunch the next day and again head to the back of the gym, but to make sure we brought something from home to eat.

So it was the next few days that, rather than head to the cafeteria for tasty, hot lunches, we headed to the small lawn behind the gym with hard-boiled eggs, fruit and, on a particularly good day, a bag of Fig Newtons-anything we could sneak out of our homes without alerting our parents or siblings that we had voluntarily given up our lunch privileges. We didn't want our families to discover our lunch arrangements because, though we had never articulated as much to one another, we felt like we were letting the racists win. To myself, I likened it to Black folks finally getting the right to go through the front door of a restaurant, but choosing to instead utilize the old backdoor Colored entrance solely because they were uncomfortable with the White folks' reaction when they exercised their right to enter through the front door. I knew we were taking the easy way out, but I rationalized that we were just innocent ninth-graders who suffered through enough day-to-day misery each school day and were, therefore, entitled to a pass to avoid, where possible, as much humiliation as we could.

One day, after we'd been by-passing the cafeteria for about a week and a half, we sat behind the gym sharing a jar of peanut butter and a sleeve of Ritz crackers. As we talked about the upcoming Florida A&M University football game, we saw the varsity basketball coach, Coach Albertson, approaching. I don't know why I had a fleeting inclination to run the other way. As he stood in front of us, I could only guess how pathetic we must have looked, especially when I noticed Mahlon had a big speck of peanut butter on the corner of his mouth and, as I stood up, I saw that I had orange cracker crumbs on my shirt.

Coach Albertson, to whom we'd never been introduced, was quite calm and successively looked us both in the eye before he said anything. "How are you guys doing today?" he asked.

"Fine, Coach," we nervously said in unison.

"I saw you guys heading behind the gym the last couple of days and decided today to check and see whether y'all were meeting girlfriends back here," said the Coach. "Anyway fellas, I can see that neither one of you should be dieting, so I don't want y'all to skip lunch anymore because both of you need nutritious meals so you can grow tall enough to someday play basketball for me."

"Ok, Coach," I said.

He looked us both in the eye again and said, "I'll see you guys later, but don't let it be back here at lunch time." He turned and walked away.

I could not help but like Coach Albertson. He had not even asked why we were skipping lunch. It was probably real clear why the two Black boys in the school were passing up lunch, but by not making us state the reason, he allowed us to retain some dignity. Mahlon and I sat there in uncharacteristic silence, lost for the moment in our own private thoughts.

When we started to leave for our next class, I said, "I guess we'll be eating with the White folk from here on in."

Mahlon, wiping the peanut butter from his mouth responded, "That's not such a bad thing I guess, 'cause I was starting to hate boiled eggs." We never skipped lunch after that day.

We got into a school routine, but never comfortable. We had to admit we were not nearly the novelty to other kids that we'd been when we first started. Lunchroom tables rarely emptied when we sat down, although we always tried to find seats that had empty seats next to them. That's not to say that all the racist students wanted to sing Kumbayah with us. Quite the contrary, a hard-core group of them still took every opportunity to let us know we were still Niggers or Coons to them. A couple of football players would say when Mahlon and I were near: "I smell a 'gar.'" The other would say "a cigar?" And the reply was: "No, a Niggah." Yet even these direct epithets were decreasing because they were not normally uttered if anyone from outside the teen Kluxsers' circle were present.
junior varsity football team and the Junior High basketball team stopped in as we and our classmates assembled for our P.E. class.

He got right to the point. "Practice for our junior high hoop team is starting Wednesday-two days from now. I'd like those of you who think you have basketball skills to come out. We have an eight game schedule and, frankly, we have to be better than we've been the past two years."

As we dispersed and began as a group to head out to the fields behind the gym, Coach Patera called out, "Mahlon and Keith, come over here!"

As we stood in front of him he smiled, "I want to personally invite you two guys to come out for the team."

Wondering why he assumed either of us could play, I said "We'll think about it, Coach."

"Good", he said, "I'll be looking for both of you on Wednesday."

I couldn't help noticing Coach Patera's swarthy complexion was almost as dark as Mahlon's. I found out later he was Cuban, like Desi Arnez. I don't know if that was the reason, but I liked Coach Patera and almost immediately decided that if Mahlon would agree, we'd be at the Wednesday practice.

I'm not proud to say, but I always noticed the coloration of people, although I did my best not to prejudge relative to character, intelligence or attractiveness. It is indisputable that the actual color of Black folks matter in perceptions of Whites towards Blacks, and indeed in perceptions of Blacks towards other Blacks. The Catholic school that had integrated the previous year, through plan or happenstance, admitted decidedly lighter-skinned Black kids. I don't know if being light-skinned made them more acceptable to White folks, but their presence in the midst of their White classmates was less startling and perhaps, as a result, less threatening.

At FHS, Mahlon, though clearly of African descent, was light complexioned; I on the other hand was dark skinned. The difference in our complexions made it easy for our classmates to distinguish the two "Colored boys." The racists spoke of Mahlon as the "Yellow One" and I was the "Black One." It should be noted here that in 1964, describing a person as Black was not a way to demographically classify an individual as the term later came to be used; rather, it was almost always a pejorative term most frequently used in my experience to demean. Unfortunately, at that time it was frequently used in the Black community for the same reason. In any event, it seemed to me that the vocal racists felt that because Mahlon obviously had some White blood flowing through his veins, he had some redeeming value. My purer Black heritage did not provide me any such value. In reaching that conclusion, I recall that Tim had told me that a couple of football players, in trying to explain why Mahlon and I were good students, had theorized that Mahlon was smart because he had White blood and I got good grades because I cheated off Nigger-lovers like him and Dietrich. In telling me that, Tim had hesitated before he used the word Nigger and his face had deeply reddened.

That Wednesday, Mahlon and I joined eleven other ninth-grade junior high hoop candidates including Tim and Stan at the outdoor hoop court behind the gym. Neither Mahlon nor I had ever played organized basketball, with most of our prior experience being occasional "pick-up" games in seventh and eighth grade P.E. classes at FAMU Junior High. As a result, the lined-up lay-up drills, standard bounce passes, jump shooting efforts, dribbling with our off hand and free-throw shooting presented real challenges for us. We noticed that these basic basketball drills seemed second nature to our White teammates who, we found out later, had played on organized teams in elementary and at the junior high school level.

Our lack of polish must have been painfully evident to Coach Patera and the surprisingly large number of on-lookers comprised for the most part of family-members including my dad. I noticed several young men whom I did not recognize standing at the far end of the court watching intently and talking animatedly among themselves. At least three had on Florida High letter jackets and they had the look of ex-high school jocks. I concluded that they were recent graduates of FHS, and I wondered why they would be interested in the first day of practice of a junior high basketball team. But then, I knew exactly why. I found myself getting more and more self-conscious of my weak basketball skills and found myself looking toward the small group of older boys at the end of the court noting that they seemed to collectively enjoy every one of the many times I missed lay-ups and free throws. I wondered whether I really wanted to play basketball with my limited skills as White people watched and critiqued.

Riding home with Dad after dropping Mahlon off, I found that some of the parents had apparently been evaluating the skill level that the two Brothers brought to the table. Dad told me that near the end of practice one of my teammate's father had come over and sat next to him. Shortly after he'd introduced himself, he, in what my dad recalled as a "paternalistic" manner, sought to console my dad by saying that I would have to get used to playing with "these guys." My dad's response was classic Lee Neyland. He told the man, "That's okay, Keith'll be fine. Those guys had better get used to playing with him." Hearing that my dad had stood up for me despite my rough obvious deficiencies was empowering. I found myself feeling that if he could believe in me, at the very least, I should believe in myself.

It did not take long for me to realize that what I lacked in fundamental basketball skills, I more than made up for with athleticism and instincts. I immediately found I could anticipate passing lanes and was quick enough to exploit them and make steals almost at will. I also had a real knack for blocking shots without fouling despite the fact that height-wise I was in the middle of the pack. My outside shot was weak, but I could score hitting lay-ups on drives and on steals where I often raced the length of the court-although I could only go right.

We had an eight-game schedule. Four were against Blessed Sacrament, the Catholic school, and two each were against Cobb Junior High and Raa Junior High. Of the eight games, all but one at Blessed Sacrament were to be played at dear old Florida High, a fact that was later clarified upon our noting the obvious: FHS had the only integrated team among the four. Going over the schedule, Mahlon said, "I guess we hardly have any away games at the all-White schools so the 'Crackers' don't riot. I guess they feel that we won't get lynched at the Catholic schools 'cause the nuns won't let 'em, especially since Blessed Sacrament has some almost-Negro kids going to school there."

After a couple of practices, I was named a starter. Mahlon, who, because he was a tenacious rebounder, I thought should have also been a starter, was to be one of the first reserves off the bench. However you viewed it, Florida High was going to have two Brothers representing one of its athletic teams. History was going to be made in the much-loved sports world of North Florida.

It was the first sports uniform I had ever worn. I loved the maroon shorts, the white and maroon jerseys emblazoned with F.H.S. Junior High, even the goofy-looking white knee socks with the maroon bands. I found to my way of thinking that while my dark skin kept me separated from the FHS student body, the uniform, nevertheless, made me feel like part of an FHS team.

Playing our first game, which happened to be against Blessed Sacrament, was a surreal experience for me. My uniform said I represented Florida High, notwithstanding my dark chocolate complexion, and the junior high cheerleaders even cheered on those relatively frequent times I scored. Of course as a team you could have kept our score with a bag of marbles-a small bag.

We won 26 to 21; I scored 15 points, mostly on drives, steals and free throws-I was 4 for 9. I guarded a guy on SC's team named Snyderburn who wasn't as quick as me but could dribble and shoot-he got 15 on me. At the end of the game, Mahlon said, "You had a little trouble guarding that White boy didn't you?"

I responded, "I know, I don't think he was really White. Man…I think he's passing."

We went on to win six out of our eight games, losing once to Cobb and, surprisingly, to BS in our one away game. I was told by Coach Patera said that we had been the best junior high record in six years.

While I'd gotten increasingly more comfortable at our home games, the experience at our away game at BS was sobering. Not only was our game played on an outside court, but it was clear that, despite the fact that Blessed Sacrament was itself integrated, Mahlon and I were still the centers of attention. Kids encircling the court seemed to point at me a lot and a couple of voices were heard calling me Sambo. I did not hear Nigger at all and frankly that in and of itself was refreshing. I was so self-conscious I continued to miss shot after shot. I looked around the crowd during a timeout. My eyes wandered and I found myself searching the crowd of students. I knew who I was looking for-her name was Carol Awkard.

I really didn't know her well at all-her dad was a professor at FAMU and her Mom, who was Filipino, was a Librarian at FAMU. Carol was gorgeous, but in thinking about whether I'd see her at the Blessed Sacrament court, I had guessed that I wouldn't be able to find her since I thought her very light complexion and straight Black hair would make her blend in too well with the White kids. I was wrong. There she was kind of standing by herself, she was close in color to most of the other students although tawnier, and she didn't seem to blend in nearly as well as I thought she would. Our eyes met and she raised her hand in a shy, little wave. I couldn't help but to wave back.

"Keith, get your head in the game!"

Embarrassed, I turned around and tried to listen to what Coach Patera was saying as we huddled around him. I couldn't stop thinking about Carol's wave.

After that time-out, I played like a crazy man scoring 12 points in the second half alone. I couldn't help it. I was showing off for a girl, something that's natural for guys to do although it was nothing I would have even thought about doing at Florida High. While I didn't really know her that well, I wanted to impress her. As the Blessed Sacrament students dispersed after the game, I didn't see her as we boarded the bus taking us back to Florida High although I couldn't have looked for her any harder.

It was kind of funny how many students spoke to me during junior high hoops season, although, most of the time, it was in the context of basketball. When the season ended, Mahlon and I once again became largely invisible to all but a very few students at FHS.

1965-66
SOPHOMORE

The summer before my tenth grade year was largely uneventful. The only problem I had with it was each day it brought me closer to a return to FHS. By the beginning of August, I was starting to count days, getting more depressed as the remaining days of freedom became fewer and fewer. I did, however, have one summer diversion-American Legion baseball. I loved the sport and we had a pretty good team made up for the most part of boys whose fathers worked at FAMU. I was a shortstop and among our best hitters; Mahlon, a lefty, was our ace, indeed, our only pitcher.

Because of our parents' affiliation with the university, we were allowed to practice on one of the college's baseball diamonds and an A&M grad student who had had low minor league experience was our coach. We practiced almost every weekday and really looked to me like a terrific team. Our only problem was, we had only one opposing team to play-a team made up of brothers who were literally from the other side of the tracks. The difference in the appearance of our two teams was telling. Though neither team had uniforms, the clothes and shoes we wore to play in were noticeably cleaner and newer than theirs. Likewise, our equipment, gloves, bats and balls looked almost brand new compared with the worn-down equipment with which they played. But given that we were the only Black American Legion baseball teams in Tallahassee, if we wanted to play games, we needed each other.

Both teams' need for the other, however, did not mask the clear tension between them. They hated and thought we "Rich Uncle Toms" who thought we were better than them; and to be truthful some of my teammates had condescendingly characterized them to one another as "those poor Niggers." We never actually fought, but their dislike of us was palpable.

A specific incident in which I was a primary actor did nothing to endear us to them. After some cajoling of our coach, I had worked my way into what had theretofore been a one-man pitching rotation: Mahlon. After insisting to everyone who'd listen and many who would not that I had a nice curveball that I could throw for strikes and after throwing a couple of simulated innings against some of our players, I was given the opportunity to start a game against our crosstown rivals.

I started the game like a young Juan Marichal-striking out two of the first three batters and getting a weak groundout. My curve was breaking sharply; I could start it tight inside and it would break across the plate-often with the batter having bailed out. The second inning, their clean-up hitter came to bat. He appeared to be a slightly older boy who happened to be physically-challenged with a metal brace supporting an atrophied leg. He always had one of his teammates serve as a proxy runner. Through several previous games, he'd earned our respect because he was a natural hitter with whip-like wrists who almost always hit the ball hard. I eyed him, wound up, and threw my only pitch. It broke sharply but outside the plate. I wound up to throw my second pitch hoping to initially direct it more inside. I was successful; it started off inside. But, to my horror, it refused to break at all. The hitter, because of his disability, could not move out of harm's way and the thud of the ball hitting his side was sickening. He grabbed his side and awkwardly tried to walk off the pain. He looked back at me with an expression reflecting anger and humiliation. It felt as though the rest of his team looked at me with only the former emotion.

I instinctively took a couple of steps toward him to apologize but he disgustedly turned away from me and hobbled to the bench as his proxy proceeded to first base. Nobody anywhere said a word. Their whole team, I felt, stared hatefully at me. I found that I could not analogize their hateful looks to those I got at Florida High because the hate they directed at me on the baseball field I felt I deserved. As it turned out, I was no more good as a pitcher after my beanball because I was afraid to start a pitch inside for fear it would stay there. We only played one more game that summer and I was back at shortstop where I belonged.

The beginning of our sophomore year brought some welcome additions to dear old FHS in the form of a couple of Black eighth-graders: Mahlon's brother, Michael, a ninth-grader, and, unbelievably, a Black girl-a pretty eleventh-grader named Elaine. It was great having others to share the diversity load with me and Mahlon. Mike, Mahlon, and I became a crew, spending lunchtime and other free time together. Elaine, a demure, fair-complexioned "girlie-girl" made friends with a few of the White girls in her class and did not hang with the brothers. She was nice, though, and we all liked her.

Academically, Mahlon and I had made a name for ourselves as good students. Mahlon was really good in math, and I, while also pretty good in math, was better in English. The Head of the English Department, Miss Carter, a lady of indeterminate age (though all guesses started in the early 60's) seemed to have trouble accepting my verbal and written abilities. Exuding Southern gentility with a maple syrupy, refined drawl, she'd asked me on two occasions if I were from New York, as if competence in the English language was beyond the grasp of Black folk from Dixie. She seemed to think I had to have been from "up north." I would tell her that while I'd been born in New York City, I grew up in Louisiana and North Carolina before coming to Tallahassee as a fourth-grader. I got a sense that she may have felt I was hiding the truth.

I had rightly or wrongly concluded that it was Miss Carter who had been "the English teacher" who had, according to Principal Bishop told him when Mahlon and I were first accepted that she did not know if she could teach Colored students. Yet, I could tell that she grew, if not to like me, at least to respect me.

Shortly before Christmas, we began reading a scene from "My Fair Lady" in class and notwithstanding all the White boys in class, Miss Carter asked me to read the part of Henry Higgens. Picture that!

Days passed into weeks. I got to know who my classmates were. Among my fellow ninth-graders, there was a small group of boys who became reasonably friendly with us. The friendliest continued to be Tim, whose father I later found out was a Math teacher at Florida High. Another guy who befriended us was Stan Dietrich, whose father was on the faculty at Florida State University.

Tim and Stan, I learned later, were the academic top of our class-literally, one and two. For that matter, those ninth-graders that dared to openly befriend us in our first few weeks at FHS usually fell into two categories: really smart and well outside of the "in-crowd" without, for all appearances, caring that they were; and city boys whose parents did not work for FSU or city government. The "smart guy" classification covered the genius-like Baker and Gareau, guys that were nice enough to us, but with whom we had little in common because they had absolutely no interest in sports.

Tim and Stan were both athletes: Tim, while lacking a tight athletic physique, was, I later found, an outstanding football player and a decent basketball player. Stan was a promising half-miler and a good hooper. In contrast, I found that the vocal racists seemed to be academically-challenged and, frequently, the progeny of blue collars and red necks. It seemed that a disproportionate number of them were football players and I always wondered why that was. Baker, Gareau and Dietrich seemed to be the type that could have sat elsewhere. Certainly their sitting next to me was but a quiet gesture of humanity; nevertheless, it spoke volumes to me. No girl ever called us a name-apparently that was inappropriate behavior under the rules of Southern belle gentility. Rather, girls for the most part treated us with absolute indifference.

Once in French, however, I was called upon to act out an introductory conversation in front of the class with a tall blond girl. When we haltingly introduced ourselves in French, she gratuitously offered her hand for me to shake, which I did. I was unnerved to find out later that she was the sister of a big football player who regularly and passionately called me Nigger.

As I look back at Florida High in 1964, I acknowledge that many of my experiences were less painful than those of Black kids who later integrated the public schools in Tallahassee because FHS, as a small demonstration school for Florida State University, had, on balance, a larger core of more racially-tolerant students given that many of their parents were highly educated instructors and professors at the university. We were undoubtedly subjected to less physical harassment. Nevertheless, as the first Blacks to attend a White high school in Tallahassee, we were, whether we wanted to be or not, pioneers of social change.

Notably, in 1964, almost nothing else in the city was integrated-not the churches, not the restaurants, not the movies, not the neighborhoods, not the doctors' offices or hospitals, except for the small Catholic elementary and junior high that had integrated the previous year, not the schools-except Florida State University, which had accepted its first Black students (one of whom had been my sister Beverly's best friend) the prior year. It did not take long, however, before I realized that the children of the faculty at FSU were not always friendly, liberal types, nor, for that matter, were kids with blue-collar parents necessarily racists.

An example comes to mind. In some of my classes there was a red-headed good "ole" boy named, Buddy Paige. He was a proud, loudly self-proclaimed "Son of Dixie." Often during class he'd make frequent gratuitous references about the South rising again, the "Damn Yankees," and to his belief in states' rights. The car that picked him up sported a Confederate flag on its bumper-a symbol that I always felt glorified a time and place where people of color were at best second-class citizens and, at worst, chattel.

If I were stereotyping based on what I thought I knew about Buddy, I would have expected him to be one who harassed me or certainly one who associated with those who did. He did neither. In one class, he chose a seat one space over from me and would quietly speak on many occasions. Not once did he disrespect or treat me as if I were invisible. He had an apparent decency about him that trumped his strong, historically conservative ideology. Buddy was one of many examples of the inaccuracy associated with stereotyping.

I was proud that Mahlon and I had to have changed some long-held stereotypes ourselves. For starters, we were always neat and clean and dressed as well, if not better, than our classmates. In addition, we spoke proper English and enunciated with some precision, especially for Southerners. As products of the all-Black Florida A&M University community, Mahlon and I had always been surrounded by college-educated adults (our fathers were both Ph.Ds) and their children who dressed and spoke like us. It did not take long, however, to realize that many of our classmates were surprised at the quality of our dress and speech.

I was once assigned to an in-class science project with a fellow student who had never spoken to me before. At the end of our week-long project, he said out of nowhere, "You know, you're not like any Colored people I've ever known before and I've known a lot of them because a bunch have worked for my dad. I mean you and the other one dress and talk mo' White than Colored."

I was caught off guard; I guess in his mind he was paying me a compliment, but something didn't seem right about it so I said, "Is that right?" He continued, "You don't act Colored at all."

I got a sense that he felt that that was the biggest compliment he could pay me; he turned and walked away. Two weeks later, the same theme played out again when one of our regular tormentors said as we walked by, "Y'all try to dress and act White, but y'all ain't gon' ever be nothing but Niggers."

I remember looking at his tired t-shirt and jeans, greasy slick black hair, and remembered that he was a tenth grader who was taking ninth grade classes. I could not get over the irony. In my mind, I had it over that guy any way you looked at it; but in his mind, he would always be better than me because no matter what, I would always be a Nigger to him. I wished he could have known that in many ways I thought he was inferior to me. That would have hurt him to no end. In retrospect, I should have told him.

Ultimately, the most joy I had dispelling a negative stereotype involved debunking the myth of the inferiority of the Black mind. Both Mahlon and I were excellent students, having been the top two students in our classes at FAMU Junior High. At FHS, we found that we were among the top students, and it seemed that even some of the teachers were surprised at that.

At the first PTA meeting that school year, which my mother, Della, and father had made a point to attend, a school administrator stated that the administration was proud to welcome its two Negro students. He then asked my parents to stand up and they were introduced. As my dad recalls, the administrator went on to say that there had not occurred any problems associated with our attendance, and that our teachers had reported that we were both excellent students. At that point, someone, later identified as being from the English Department, stated, "Keith has even made an 'A' in English."

I've learned through the years that there must be something in my dad's DNA that makes him unable to allow even the smallest perceived racial slight to go unchallenged. He stood up. "Keith's a good all-around student, so I don't know what your comment that he even made an 'A' in English is supposed to mean?'"

According to my dad, a silence ensued, reflecting a collective embarrassment. As my dad continued to stand awaiting a response, the administrator who had welcomed my parents stood up. "I think Dr. Neyland, that all that was intended by that comment was that ninth grade English is a tough subject for virtually all ninth-graders and 'A's' are few and far between." Dad said, "Okay, I was just wondering," and sat down.

As I look back at that incident, I've realized that it was possible that the statement by the English teacher may have been totally innocuous. I doubt that it was, however, given that Principal Bishop had advised my dad that someone in the English Department had complained before the school year began that she did not know if she could teach Colored students. I have since concluded that holding a little refutable paranoia on the way Whites perceive and treat Black folk is healthy.

In any event, the incident at that PTA meeting was one of countless examples that demonstrated that when it came to standing up to White folks on issues of race, I was swimming upstream to be like my dad. But after he told me the PTA story, I resolved to swim harder.

On the subject of PTA meetings, I remember hearing about another incident at one that lends itself to recounting here. While my parents regularly attended PTA meetings, Mahlon's mother attended less frequently and his father never did. On Mrs. Rhaney's first such visit, which she made with my parents, as she stood near the punch bowl during the post-meeting punch and cookie "meet and greet," a mother of one of our schoolmates approached her warmly and introduced herself. Perhaps I should mention here that Mrs. Rhaney, who was from Cuba, looked as White as anybody in the room.

Anyway, after the introduction, the lady leaned in a little closer in something of a conspiratorial mode and said with barely controlled indignation, "Do you believe that they have Colored boys at this school now?"

Mrs. Rhaney looked at the woman and with her distinctive Spanish accent said sweetly, "My son is Colored." I don't know what the woman said or did after Mrs. Rhaney set her straight, but that's just as well. It's probably sweeter to just imagine the extent of her embarrassment.

At school, me and the Rhaney boys started to drop our guard with a couple of our classmates-namely Tim and Stan. We even reached the point where we (Mahlon, Mike ,and I) began "playing the dozens" with each other in their presence talking about each other's mother as we had at FAMU High. You could tell when I would say something about their mother being ugly or that she'd left some of her clothes at my room or they might come back suggesting the same type of thing about my mom or that she was fat, Tim and Stan initially looked puzzled until they realized that Black boys for some odd reason thought playing the dozens was fun. The topper came one day when Stan, out of nowhere, told Tim in our presence to tell his (Tim's) mom to stop calling him (Stan) at home asking if she could visit; it was getting to be a problem. Notably, we never played the dozens across racial lines and, thankfully, the "game" had a short shelf life at FHS.

In early October, Mahlon and I were awaiting basketball season. We were prepared to move up to junior varsity and waiting for the official word from Coach Thomas, the JV coach, that we had made the team. Waiting anxiously with us was a new arrival at the school. His name was Lonnie Groot and he'd come to FHS from North Carolina. Lonnie honestly did not seem to notice that Mahlon and I were not White like him. He took to us, especially me, like we were related. He ate lunch with us, talked to us between classes and had even come to my house for a visit-something even Tim and Stan had not done up to that point.

Lonnie was just a good guy who apparently did not have a prejudiced bone in his body. Moreover, he shared a love for one of Mahlon's and my favorite things-basketball. When I first saw him play in P.E. on a day it was too rainy to go outside, I saw that he had a nice little game. While not particularly quick, he handled the ball smoothly and if he got open out to 17 feet or so, his shot was money. Just as I sized his game up, I sensed that he was evaluating mine. While he was unquestionably a better shooter than me, particularly if he were not closely guarded, I was noticeably quicker with a quick first step that enabled me to drive to the basket almost at will, though I could only go right.

When as it turned out we played a half-court game, we wound up guarding each other. I got to the basket on him with no problem at least partially because he had little interest in playing defense. He lived to score the basketball; and when he got a couple of good screens from Mahlon who was on his team, he could put it down. But the difference was, I played defense with a passion-always. For some reason I undertook the challenge of trying to stop my man from scoring. Looking back, my compulsion to play such tenacious defense may have had its genesis when Phil Snyderburn lit me up in the first Blessed Sacrament junior high game. I had been embarrassed and, I guess, from that game on I played defense not to be embarrassed. I tried to deny my man the ball, guarded him closely when he had it, seriously contested his every shot, and always played the passing lanes looking, with frequent success, for steals.

On the day that basketball practice started, Mahlon, Lonnie and I were shooting with a dozen other guys waiting on Coach Thomas to pull our JV team together. I looked at the other end of the gym where the varsity players, looking so much cooler and skilled than our group, were shooting and casually talking to one another. Out of the corner of my eye, I saw Coach Albertson come out of the locker room and noticed, surprisingly, that he turned and walked in our direction. Seeing him walk in our direction, I tried to act nonchalant but the 15-foot shot I took as he approached missed everything.

"Keith, come here a second," he said. Slowly I walked over.

He looked me in the eyes and said, "Keith, you're going to be playing varsity this year." At first I didn't know if I truly understood what he was saying.

"Go over and join the varsity at the other end of the gym and I'll be down there in a minute," he said.

I started what felt like a walk through wet cement toward my new teammates. I had not been prepared for this and I could tell from no longer hearing bouncing balls from the basket at which the JV players were shooting that they were silently watching me make that meaningful walk.

As a sophomore, with just one year of organized ball, I had made the varsity hoop team. I didn't know whether to be happy or scared to death; I think I experienced equal parts of both emotions. This was going to be one of my biggest challenges and I was going to face it by myself.

The leap from junior high ball to varsity was huge. The varsity players were so much more skilled and so much bigger. At just about 5'10", I was one of the two shortest guys on the team. I noticed that several of them were really good shooters and after a few lay-up drills, I realized that everyone on the team could comfortably make left-handed layups except me. All of the players were pretty nice though. From that first day when I moved up to varsity, they made me feel at home with them and welcomed me into the varsity locker room. Yet moving to the varsity locker room was less of a big deal than moving out of the outer locker room where the JV players dressed.

I knew Mahlon was genuinely happy for me. He had whispered to me, "Man, you big time now." And I'm sure several other JV players were happy I'd moved up if for no other reason than it would mean more playing time for them. But Lonnie's congratulations rung hollow. I sensed that he either thought he, too, should have made varsity, or that I shouldn't have. Whatever he thought, our friendship was never what it had been starting out.

All in all, it was a tough season. As the only Black varsity basketball player in the North Florida panhandle, I was the star attraction (at least for shouted epithets, ridicule and derision) for the fans of the teams we played at home and, on an exponentially worse basis, on the road. As we played teams in the little Redneck towns within a 50-mile or so radius of Tallahassee, I found a true, frequently terrifying, isolation when our team first ran on the floor to start doing our layup drills. I would be the only person of color in the gym and in virtually every gym we played verbal missiles were launched at me by a bunch of students and older folk (I guessed parents and relatives of players). They yelled Nigger, Coon, "Rastus," "Jungle Bunny," "Sambo"-you get the picture. A couple times I was called "Meadowlark" (who I suppose everybody knew was the most famous Globetrotter) I guess by a more liberal faction not into shouting racial epithets. In any event, it was brutal. I was not being self-conscious and projecting that people were focused on me; in other words, I didn't have "Rabbit Ears." The hateful bigots were unquestionably pouring their pent-up, historically-held hatred on the narrow shoulders of a lone 15-year old boy-me

I could not wait for the games to end so I could get out of the threatening, degrading environments in which I found myself each and every away game. I wondered what my teammates thought; I wondered what Coach Albertson thought. But, unbelievably, no one ever spoke to me about the treatment I was receiving.

What made matters worse was that along with being a soul brother on the team, I was also a "pine brother" since I regularly rode the bench during game time. I only got in games in extreme situations-when we were winning by a lot or losing by a lot. I accepted that the guys that played ahead of me, though not my equal in athleticism, were better overall basketball players. I did, however, get in the first home game we played which was at home versus West Bainbridge (GA) High School. We were up 15 points or so with around 3 minutes to go when Coach Albertson beckoned to me and told me to go in for our star guard Bruce Gilchrist.

When I ran to the scorer's table, a murmur audibly rose with the West Bainbridge crowd. As I ran on the court to take the ball out, unfortunately right in front of the Georgia fans, an adult voice yelled out, "The Klan is gonna get you boy." I had barely been in the game 30 seconds when I caught a pass at the top of the key, I immediately did the one thing I did fairly well: I drove to my right toward the basket, past my defender. One of their taller players cut my route off to the hoop so I dribbled to my right further away from the basket and I guess in a "What the hell" mode I threw up a ridiculous sweeping hook. It went in-nothing but net. I heard a good-sized cheer from the FHS fans. My first varsity points-the first points ever scored for old FHS by a student who was not White. I don't know where that hook came from, I'd not been known to feature such a shot, but who knows maybe I was the next coming of Meadowlark.

One of the two worst places I played as far as racial abuse was Monticello (Perry was the other), a town about 26 miles outside of Tallahassee. That crowd in their little band-box gym was really enraged to see the integrated FHS team take the court. We had had to wait just off the court for the Black janitor to finish his back and forth dry-mopping. As we waited, a man in a coat and tie who obviously was a principal or some other authority figure at the school stared directly at me. As I looked back, his facial expression seemed to harden with a look that clearly said he was not happy I was there. It was beyond clear that I was not welcomed by anybody at Monticello High.

The crowd stood up to get a better look at me as we stood there. I felt some solace in seeing the Black janitor. I wasn't by myself. As he walked off past us, I was hoping to at least get a supportive look from the brother, but he pointedly avoided eye-contact with me and actually seemed scared as he hustled past. I was alone here even if he was present. The game itself was the toughest I had to endure that year. As visitors, our bench was right in front of their student section. I was a Nigger or worse all night. But that wasn't all. In the second quarter, something hit me on my head-a spitball. Then came a couple more. The teammate of mine sitting on my left (I was on the end) noticed the fairly steady stream of spitballs and moved further to his left leaving a space between him and me and effectively isolating me to be a better target. I would probably been layered in spitballs at the end of the game if a vicious fight had not broken out on the court. For what was probably only seconds seemed to me like an eternity as both benches cleared with guys swinging away. I instinctively felt that I'd better move away from my spitball-throwing tormenters so I stepped out on the court as the fight ensued.

Suddenly I was grabbed around my shoulders. In a split second, I felt sure I was about to get seriously beat up. I can't describe the sense of relief I felt when I saw that the person who had wrapped his arms around me was Coach Albertson. He kept me in his grasp until the huge uniformed State Trooper (who I later heard had not been at games until word that the integrated Demons were coming to town) cleared the fight up. After the fight, Coach Albertson set me down next to him for the rest of the spitball-free game. Monticello was the worst.

I probably got the most exposure, however, when we played Leon High, the biggest school in Tallahassee. Leon would have been our biggest rival in basketball if we had ever beaten them; but as it stood, we were historically just their punching bag. We played them twice a season, home and away and, for some reason, the home games were always played in Florida State University's Tully gym-I guess so that more people could watch, kind of like the huge crowd the lions used to get when they were fed Christians. Anyway, as expected, we started getting brutalized early and often. At halftime we were down 46-23. Halfway through the third quarter, Coach Albertson summoned me from my trusty perch at the end of the bench and told me to get in there for Gilchrist. As I went to the scorer's table, the Leon crowd almost as one increased the volume of their on-going game din. I didn't hear a chorus of epithets, though I heard some, their crowd just got louder with anticipation. The first time I ran up the court, something whizzed by my face. Somebody had thrown a coin from the crowd-that was a first. The refs didn't stop play and I was unaware of any other missiles coming out of the stands.

For whatever reason, given in Tully gym I was on the biggest stage by far than any I'd ever played on, I was comfortable-even relaxed. I hit a jumper from the corner and later a driving lay-up on which I was fouled and hit the free throw. FHS was beat that night 84-59, but it might not have been that close if I hadn't contributed my season-high five points.

I was glad when the basketball season ended. Away games had almost always taken a psychological toll on me. I wasn't certain what I wanted to do, if anything, in the way of Spring sports. Mahlon and Michael, conveniently a pitcher and catcher combination, were going out for the baseball team. I was a bit reluctant to follow them to the diamond for two reasons: I had a crippling fear of getting beaned by an opposing red-neck pitcher and I happened to be the fastest guy in my class. So balancing my fear of a beaning against my relatively big-time speed, I decided to go out for track.

Track was a pretty big deal at FHS-maybe bigger than baseball. We practiced and competed on the same tack as FSU's team; and it was located only around fifty yards or so from our school. I didn't know what event I'd focus on, although I figured that as a Black male it was my mandate to run the hundred yard dash-a race that always seemed to be top-heavy with Black folk. I also, for some reason, had an interest in the high jump, an event I'd never tried. From day one, our coach-Coach Therman, a young very-tanned athletic-looking guy, threw me in with the 440 and 880 guys. That group was constantly assigned to run sets of 220s almost at full speed over and over-after one was completed, we'd walk back across the field to where we'd originally started and run another. There were seven of us in this group and we'd run sets of six 220s and then jog around the track and start another set of six.

The first couple of days I was truly dragging butt. As I started to get in track shape (there's a huge difference in basketball and track shape), however, I found that I was starting to fall into a natural stride as we ran that facilitated my maintenance of speed and mitigated against the onset of fatigue. Soon, I found that fairly effortlessly I was staying near the front of the pack as we ran, although I was cognizant of not drawing undue attention to myself by trying to regularly lead the group.

The first track meet we were scheduled to run that year was at Robert E. Lee High School in Jacksonville, some three hours away by bus. I was told that in my first track competition as a varsity track guy, I was going to be a member of the sprint-medley relay and that I would run the third leg which covered the weird distance of 330 yards. My fellow relay members were: Doug Mullins, a short star running-back who had an okay hundred time who would start us off in the hundred, Barry Handberg (who at a 9.6 in the hundred may have been the fastest White track high school athlete in the country) who was also short with a mop haircut covering the next 220 yards, yours truly handling the 330, and James White, our top 880 man bringing us home on the last 440.

Over and over we practiced passing the baton until we were soon efficient in our exchanges. I was excited to be a Florida High trackster and a member of our sprint medley team. For some reason, I had a sense of belonging. Shortly after we got off the bus at Robert E. Lee High I found that my sense of belonging had been largely illusory. It was around 12:30 when we were quickly ushered to the school cafeteria for lunch. The cafeteria was huge, maybe ten times or more larger than the one at FHS. It seemed to be packed with hundreds of students-all WHITE students. For some reason, despite its name, I had assumed that Robert E. Lee High School would be integrated, especially in the third biggest city in Florida. It was not. I was the only Black student in the massive room- It felt like my first visit to Florida High's cafeteria times ten.

Perhaps sensing my thoughts, Coach Therman walked over to me as I stood next to Stan and said, "Come on, Keith and Stan, let's get something to eat." He walked with us through the line. All the hair-netted food-servers on the line were White and largely ignored me. However, I noticed through the glass windows in the doors to the kitchen behind the servers, the heads of two Black women, presumably cooks, smiling broadly, then waving at me. They seemed glad to see me-no, I thought, they seemed *proud* to see me. I quickly waved back as I pushed my tray along. "Wow!" I thought. Maybe this integration stuff was bigger than my day-to-day hell.

Extrapolating from the sheer joy in the eyes of the two cooks, I realized that lots of Black people were proud of what we integration pioneers were doing. It was bigger than us, we were standing for something. I felt strengthened to face the challenge waiting for me as I sat down in the cavernous cafeteria filled with Caucasians. Let 'em look, I felt empowered because I did not think about the discomfort I would feel sitting there eating my lunch. Rather, for once, I concentrated on being a hero of my people-like Gandhi or Martin Luther King as ridiculous as that may sound. I had to think big to quell the fear in the pit of my stomach as I saw students pointing and looking at me. I drank from a carton of milk, as the new imagery of me as an instrument of social change revolved in my mind; I felt oddly at peace.

The track meet was that evening under the lights. We were competing against a large contingent from Robert E. Lee and another smaller Jacksonville high school; Lee had two, sometimes three, runners in all the individual races, and two teams in all the relay races. It seemed like everywhere you looked on the track and its infield the gray (of course, the colors of the Generals of R.E. Lee High would include gray) and burgundy uniforms of the strutting, highly confident Lee Generals were abundantly present. There was a sizable crowd in the stands, cheerleaders from the local schools were doing their thing trying to act pumped and some members of the Lee band played loudly in the corner of the bleachers.

Robert E. Lee was serious about their track program and it showed. Nevertheless, we beat them like Grant beat their namesake. Things started badly for them in the first race, the 100-yard dash. Barry Handburg ran a 9.8 that won by 5 yards, a mile in the hundred yard dash. Mullins came in third. We came in second and third in the 440 (the winning time was 52.8) and we won the 880. Stan Dietrich, who as a sophomore was our best miler, was nipped for first in the mile; and Barry ran away with the 220. They took first and second in the low hurdles and we came in second in the mile relay.

By the sprint medley relay, we were feeling pretty good about ourselves and the Lee Generals were strutting noticeably less. There were five teams in the medley relay –two from Lee, two from the other high school and one comprised of FHS Demons. The 330 guys were set in our lanes as the gun went off starting the 100-yard leg. In that short race, run for us by Mullins, it looked as if the baton changes of all teams were pretty close. I could see clear separation, however, when Barry took the baton for his 220 leg and started coming toward me. Boy, that short, little guy was fast. I could see that we had a serious lead of about seven yards when I took off and reached my right hand back. The exchange was seamless.

I took off low and hard. I made myself think of this 330 as just a little longer 220 and I knew I could run the hell out of a 220. I could feel my stride kick in and I was moving gracefully, almost floating. As I came toward our anchorman for the 440 yard leg, I saw him take off with his right hand back-our exchange was smooth and he was gone. We wound up winning by 10 yards with a time 1½ seconds better than the school's record. The four of us hugged each other-not many teams are more dependent on one another than a track relay team. We knew that each one of us had done our job.

Coach Therman announced to us that we had broken the FHS Sprint medley record by 2.5 seconds. He then pulled me aside and joyously told me that I had run a great 330 leg and had increased our lead by three yards. "You know, Keith, there's no open 330 yard race and since we got Barry winning all the 220s, I think I'm going to look at you in the quarter. On Monday, I want you to come out and run a quarter for time. Let's see exactly what you're working with."

As I got on the bus for our ride back to Tallahassee, Barry said as I walked by, "There's our Nubian warrior." I didn't know how I should feel with that label, although I knew Barry wasn't a racist. So I just smiled. I didn't have the faintest idea what Nubian meant. When I got home and asked my dad to explain-I embraced the name. On that team, I guess, I was their Nubian warrior, I'd certainly been called worse.

The following Monday was starkly overcast. I was nervous because it was clear from the various comments to me that everybody knew and, for one reason or another, was anxious to see my time trial in the quarter. I realized that among the most anxious were Jim Long and Joe Fixel, the two incumbent quarter milers on the team. At the track, we ran some 100-yard wind sprints on the track's infield. I noticed that it was one of those rare days when we had the track to ourselves-no FSU track guys were around. After we'd all loosened up, Coach Therman loudly announced, "OK fellas, we've got a quarter-mile time trial to run. Are you ready, Keith?"

I looked at him and nodded. "You don't seem too enthused," he said, smiling.

"I'm ready, Coach," I said, trying to sound like I was.

The whole track team stood around Coach Therman, who was holding a stopwatch at the start/finish line of the quarter. I stepped out on the track. I wasn't using starting blocks as quarter guys do in real races; I bent over slightly ready to take off. Coach Therman dramatically yelled, "On your mark, set, GO!" I started out low and hard; by the first turn, I hit my stride-I was moving and I felt good. Running this race just seemed to come naturally. It felt surreal, running alone against the gray sky. Even as I ran, I wondered what this lone Black boy must look like running by himself as White folks watched. I later thought with a smile, at least they had not been running after me. I kept a strong stride up the back stretch and used my flowing momentum to sling me through the last curve. I knew this was the time-right around the 330 yard mark that the "Bear" waited to jump on the backs of tiring quarter milers. I started to feel a little tightening in my chest but determined to stride it out—not fight it-so that I didn't tighten up. I didn't want my teammates to see me struggling as I brought it in. As a Nubian Warrior, I had to proudly stride in and I did just that.

I was not that tired as Coach Therman and my teammates crowded around. Looking at his stop watch, he announced, "Without starting blocks, and running, no striding, by himself for the first time in the quarter, he's run a 52.1. That ties the best quarter we've had in competition in two years. Keith, my boy, you're officially a quarter-miler." I didn't know what I should feel.

My high jumping skills were less developed. We had an eleventh grade high jumper named, Kent Deeb, a handsome, somewhat dark-complexioned guy who I believe was of Lebanese heritage. He was just a bit shorter than me and was known as a very good football player despite his relative small size. He was one of the best dressers at FHS and rarely seemed to ever have a hair out of place even at practice. He was also, technique-wise, a very good Class B high jumper. While I struggled to clear higher than 5'8", Kent sometimes jumped 6 and above. While his beating me hurt my pride, I couldn't get my technique down well enough to do anything about it. In any event, he was nice about consistently beating my rear end and, probably because he accurately concluded early on that I was no threat, he regularly tried to help me improve my technique.

My high jumping "skill" somehow got me invited to Gainesville to compete in the highly-regarded Florida Relays, one of the most prestigious college and high school track competitions in the South. Track guys from all high school sizes throughout Florida and a few from south Georgia were invited to compete at the U of F's track if they met the participatory standards. From FHS, Barry was there with one of the fastest hundred times in the country; Stan just made it with his mile time; James White just made it with his best 880 time; and my 5'8" best high jump was the minimum height that got a high jumper in. Kent, who unlike me, would have had a legitimate reason to be there for the high jump was nursing a muscle pull.

My teammates and I had come in one car driven by Coach Therman, and we planned to return to Tallahassee later that afternoon. When I got there in my FHS track uniform and sweats, I immediately went over to the high jump pit. I noticed bunches of tall, loose-limbed jumpers milling around and stretching. Two of them, one from a Georgia high school and one from Miami had placed the bar, I heard them say, at 5'8." As the other jumpers continued to stretch and appeared to half-heartedly pay attention-the Georgia kid and the one from Miami, in succession, ran to the bar and oh-so-casually cleared it.

I might have been able to handle their display of prowess had they removed their sweat suits before they had jumped. Of course, they had chosen not to and I was no good after watching their show. When the competition started, I took three tries at the starting height of 5'8" and missed badly on each. Nothing like a little humility to keep your feet on the ground which, unfortunately, is not a good place for a high jumper to be.

I found Coach Therman in the infield and he and I watched Barry in the hundred. I assumed that Barry had a good chance of losing given that there were a couple of brothers in the hundred finals (conclusive evidence, by the way, that integration had not fully kicked in). I should not have doubted it.

Barry's 9.5 nipped one of the Soul Brothers at the finish line. I was happy my White teammate had won. I had to take a moment to let that resonate-but I was. My buddy Stan was among the last milers to finish, as was James , our half-miler, in his race. We were not surprised with our finishes; except for Barry, we Class B guys rarely successfully competed with the studs from the big schools in our state.

My first open quarter was two weeks later at the P.K. Youngue Relays in Gainesville. P. K. Youngue High School was the equivalent of FHS since it was the University of Florida's demonstration school. Like FHS, it was a Class B school and its relays were the biggest Class B competition other than the state tournament which was also in Gainesville but on the University of Florida track. For a high school, P.K. Youngue had an outstanding track. With Barry, of course we made an early splash-he won the 100 in 9.5, his best time ever and one of the best times in the country that year. (Later that year he got a full track scholarship to the U of F)

A couple of races later, it was my turn in the quarter mile. There were eight guys in the race representing eight Class B schools. Because I had not run a competitive quarter, I had the bad fortune to be in lane eight, the outside lane, which, based on the quarter's staggered start, meant that I would start off way ahead of my competitors and wouldn't really see them (unless some of them were world-class) until we hit the 330 turn. I crouched down in my starting position in the blocks.

It seemed like I was the only one in the race because of the stagger-but then I'd had some recent experience running the quarter by myself. I got a good start out of the blocks, and ran hard as I motored down the back stretch. I couldn't tell where I was in relation to my competitors. But as I ran, I was aware of my passing two students standing right next to the track. I clearly heard one say to the other as I ran by, "Look at that Nigger go." Talk about race commentary. Given that I was the only person of color in the race, I concluded that, while I couldn't verify it by sight, I must have been doing pretty well. I won the quarter in 51 flat and broke the quarter-mile record of the P.K. Youngue Relays.

Because of my success in the quarter, I looked forward to running it at the Conference Regional Finals held at our track. I knew I would be the favorite particularly since the schools in our conference had relatively weak track programs. I envisioned running away from my competitors. The day before the meet, however, Coach Therman delivered some sobering news. He advised me that he was going to run Barry in his normal hundred and 220, but had decided to run him also in MY quarter. As if that wasn't enough, he went on to say that he'd also decided to take me out of the mile relay I was to anchor and, instead, run me against Barry in all three races. I couldn't even fake a positive reaction to this news. Now, rather than high-stepping it in for victories in the quarter and the mile-relay, I was looking-at best-at three seconds.

While Coach Therman further stated that he had decided to assign the races as he'd advised me because it gave him more flexibility in how he assigned races to us for State, I couldn't help but feel this was Barry's idea so that he could get three firsts in three individual races. Whatever the reason, I knew I wouldn't be crossing a finish line first the next day.

In Hollywood, the underdog against all odds can sometimes step up and dramatically win something that nobody thought him capable of winning. However, after we finished the hundred, I realized how far I was from "Hollywood." I hadn't embarrassed myself, but it did feel like Barry had beaten me like a "runaway slave." He ran a pedestrian (for him) 9.8 and I came in with an OK 10.1. No realistic surprise that he beat me, and I felt a little better when I realized that I came in well-ahead of the guy who finished third. Shortly after the hundred, I found myself adjusting my blocks for the start of what used to be my race-the quarter. As fate would have it, Barry was in the lane next to me on my right and because of the stagger, slightly ahead of me.

I knew Barry had never run a competitive quarter, but that didn't give me much confidence since I also knew he had incredibly fast times in the 220. To me this little guy was otherworldly fast-I gave myself zero chance to win. Beating Barry in the quarter could have been a better Hollywood finish to me than if I'd won the hundred. When the race ended, however, I realized I was still in Tallahassee. Barry had won-but the race was not without its drama. When the gun sounded starting the race, Barry took off like a jet. I could see him steadily pulling away from me as he traversed the first curve and hit the backstretch. He was well ahead of me running like he was running a hundred-yard dash-arms furiously pumping, short, little legs moving in blurs. I settled into my racing stride and, pretty much, settled into a mindset for coming in second. When Barry hit around bear country at the 330 mark, I started seeing chinks in his armor. I could see by the way his head began tilting slightly backward and his arm swing and running gait became more jerky that the bear, one of the real fat ones, had seen him coming and jumped on his back.

My whole frame of mind changed. Something akin to a predatory instinct took over. The fact that Barry was obviously tightening up made him vulnerable to my overtaking him even though he was well ahead. I picked up my stride and could see myself cutting down the distance between us. With about fifty yards for Barry to go, I was at least 15 yards behind him. Even running as hard as I could, I could still tell that he was struggling mightily. I kept coming-gaining on him with each stride. When he was about 20 yards from the finish line, I saw him glance to his left as if he knew I was gaining. I saw that his face was distorted in a vein-popping mask of pain. Inside of 10 yards to the finish line I was but two yards behind him. Drawing strength from God knows where, and showing an almost super-human will to win, he actually lunged at the finish line and dropped almost like he'd been shot. He lay on the track facedown not trying to get up, but struggling to catch his breath.

I walked over to him, and by that time, Coach Therman and several of our teammates had him surrounded and he'd rolled over on his back. When he saw me looking down on him, he said between gasping, ragged breaths, "I will never ever run that race again. Keith, it's all yours."

Two of his teammates gingerly helped him up and he, standing between them, put his arms on their shoulders as they supported his halting walk to the track's infield.

Coach Therman walked over to me. "Well, Keith, you'll be my only runner in the 220," he said. "I realize now why short guys don't tend to run the quarter-their shorter strides make them work too hard. That almost killed Barry. Are you feeling OK?"

"I'm ready, Coach," I said.

I was. I won the 220 by 5 yards. With my second to Kent in the high jump (I cleared 5'8"; he won with 5'10") I was the high scorer of the meet.

State Championship

Next, we headed again to Gainesville, but this time it was for the State Championships at the University of Florida's track and field-by far the biggest deal in Florida High School. It was such a big deal that funds had been put up for the team to go down to Gainesville Friday night so that we could be fully rested for the meet the next morning.

Staying at a motel, eating in a restaurant and going to a movie-as promised by Coach Therman-did not have nearly the appeal to me as it had to the rest of my teammates. Despite the presence of the University of Florida, to me, Gainesville had a distinctly small-town, red-neck atmosphere. I don't know if the "powers" set up an itinerary with the integrated status of our track team in mind (because in 1966 there were still restaurants, motels, and movie theaters where Black folks were not welcomed and they were made to know that they were not welcomed), but we had a thankfully uneventful dinner at a Howard Johnsons where we were to also stay.

At the movie theater, I got some serious stares and a couple of not-so-subtle fingers pointed my way but heard no derogatory names-although I had kind of developed a knack for not hearing epithets to protect my sensitivities. At that time, I had never been to a White theater in the South before. The movie, "Hush Hush Sweet Charlotte" was not one I would have picked; it was, however, objectively better than the Mantan Molan movies I had regularly watched at the all-Black Leon theater back in Tallahassee.

Lodging arrangements were definitely made more complicated by having me around. I know Stan would have been OK rooming with me, but as it turned out, each room was to sleep three boys-two in twin beds and one in a cot. I can only imagine the machinations that Coach Therman and the other chaperoning adults had to exercise to find two boys willing to room with a dreaded Black boy. I'm sure when Coach Therman contemplated becoming a coach, he had not envisioned that he might have to also dabble so much in Sociology, especially race-relations. Anyway the brave souls (or the ones that drew the short straws), were Barry and Mullins. I didn't think Barry would have minded so much rooming with me, he was a smart guy who kind of marched to his own beat. Mullins, on the other hand, had never been ugly in any way to me, basically just for the most part, ignoring me. But as a star football player, he did pal around with the biggest racists on the football team.

The evening went OK. You can probably guess who got the cot, but that was not a problem given their upperclassman status. I do recall before we turned off the light to go to sleep that Mullins said, "Now Keith, you don't have to go around telling folks we were roommates." He paused, trying to make himself laugh. "Especially people like Duke and Mike Peece."

He tried to play everything off as if he were joking, but I knew he wasn't joking and he knew I knew he wasn't joking. Course, I wouldn't have said anything to those two Kluxxers if I saw them getting ready to walk off the rim of the Grand Canyon, except maybe, after an appropriate pause, yelling, "HAPPY LANDING!"

I didn't sleep well that Friday night and the morning appeared too soon-cloaked in a beautiful sunrise and a stomach full of queasiness. I was nervous, more nervous than I'd ever been over a sporting event. I knew I was expected by Coach Therman, my team, and more importantly my family to be in close contention, if I didn't win. However, I couldn't stop concentrating on the fact that the state meet was open only to runners that had the best times in competition that year. Thinking about that caused some self-doubt to compromise my affirmative efforts to make myself believe I was confident. I knew that I could lose and maybe lose badly.

Under those circumstances, I would no longer be my team's Nubian Warrior; I would just be their Colored teammate. I thought to myself in a moment of race pride that's OK. Being only a Nubian was still something about which I was eminently proud; but I liked the thought of having warrior-status. As a Black Warrior, up against so many White competitors, I was determined to do the warrior thing by leaving it all on the battlefield or more accurately, the University of Florida's track.

I stood tall; I told myself I was in it to win it. As the team nervously climbed onto the bus; I found that my self-generated pep talk had had one discernible benefit, the butterflies were no longer swarming in my stomach.

Unlike the Florida Relays, that day at the state meet I was feeling a boatload of pressure. As the meet started, I high-jumped 5'8," which surprisingly got me a third in that event. Barry, to no one's surprise, snatched the 100-yard dash with a crisp 9.7.

After Stan came in third in the Mile and FHS was shut out in the hurdles, it was time for the open quarter. I found myself in Lane 4, which let me know that I had the fourth best official Class B time that year. I had not heard of the guys in Lanes 2 and 3, but I certainly knew of the tall smug-looking guy in Lane 1-Hamilton Jarvis, the incumbent Class B 440-yard champ. I'd heard he'd already received a partial scholarship offer in track from FSU. He was the "cream of the crop," and he had an air about him that made it clear that he was aware of his status and knew that the rest of us were aware, too.

As I stood at my starting blocks, I glanced over in his direction and for an uncomfortable moment we just stared before he wrinkled his nose up as if he smelled a foul odor and looked away.

I had just been ready to nod a respectful hello to him and upon his snub, I felt an uncontrollable wave of anger that replaced the anticipatory pressure I'd been experiencing. Ok, Ham Jarvis had just slighted a Nubian warrior, and for that moment, I stopped thinking about being the first to cross the finish line and started thinking solely about beating his arrogant ass.

I stretched as I got into the starting blocks. For practice, I bolted from my blocks for a practice start. I had timed it by watching out of the corner of my eye Ham practice-starting from his blocks. When he took off, I did too. He ran about ten yards; I, for some reason, felt the need to run twelve. I wanted him to see me ahead of him if only in a practice start. I couldn't believe my otherwise passive butt was trying to engage in gamesmanship with the fastest Class B guy in the state. I felt good as I stretched into the blocks for the start of the open quarter. As we crouched in the blocks and raised up, primed to take off at the crack of the gun, I-if nobody else-knew that I was someone to be reckoned with.

At the sound of the gun, I took off like I thought I was running the hundred. For a split second, I could feel myself stumbling and frantically tried to regain my balance. As I regained it, I knew that I had lost a yard or two to Ham and the guys in lanes 2 and 3.

At the first curve, I hit my stride. I was going fast but I was determined to remain relaxed. It helped that I really didn't know where I was relative to the others because of the stagger. I tried to keep my form as I went as fast as I could while knowing the bear hung out at the 330 mark waiting for quarter-milers who failed to save a little something in the tank to take them home. That was my mindset: go as fast as I could with the most relaxed stride I could maintain. My stride seemed to lengthen.

As we reached the curve leading to the straight-away to the finish line, I saw that Ham was a couple of yards ahead of me in Lane

1, and I was in second. It was a two-man race. I felt pretty strong and he certainly did not look to be struggling-even then I could see he was a smooth runner. This race was coming down to one thing-speed. The faster of us would win.

I saw it with 30 yards to go: I was faster than him. I caught him and passed him and broke the tape a yard ahead of him as the Class B State champ in the quarter.

I could not have been happier, although you couldn't really tell because I stayed bent over at the waist trying to catch my breath. I looked over at Lane 1 and there was Ham crying as he was being comforted by a man who appeared to be his coach. For a split second, I debated walking over to tell him he'd run a good race, but I thought better of it. It helped that I was pretty certain that had he won, he wouldn't have said a damn thing to me. Instead, I thought about how happy my family was going to be-especially my dad-to have a State champion, a sophomore state champion, in the house.

1966-67
JUNIOR

My junior year began with much less drama at dear old Florida High. The name-calling was hardly a big deal to us anymore, and, to be honest, had virtually ceased except for a few die-hard senior football players who still found ways to get an epithet in from time to time. As the school year progressed into October, one day I was summoned out of Chemistry class to the Principal's office.

In his office, Principal Bishop asked me before I sat down, "Keith, you and Mahlon doing OK?"

"Yes sir," I responded, noticing that he seemed unusually nervous.

Directing me to sit down, he quickly got to what was on his mind. "Look, Keith, I remember telling you and Mahlon when you guys were first admitted that we did not want y'all to play football and basketball; and you both ignored this directive with respect to basketball and became stars." He smiled at me to let me know that our playing basketball had, in the administration's view, ultimately worked out okay.

With his smile disappearing he continued. "We seriously did not want you to play football because we could not protect you from potentially violent incidents in that inherently rough game. Now...," he paused and looking almost sheepish continued. "I can't honestly say that things are a lot better now, but...well according to Coach Rose, you have outstanding aptitude for the game with your speed and elusiveness that he's seen in your Phys. Ed. classes. And frankly Keith, Coach Rose wanted me to extend an invitation to you to come out for the football team."

Caught totally off-guard, I didn't immediately respond. He continued, "I know this sounds a bit crazy, given that our team has already played two games. But according to Coach Rose, you have special talent that could allow you to contribute right away. It won't be easy if you decide to go out for the team; I know the ugly slurs you hear in away basketball games and I can't honestly say that at football games it won't be worse; but if you go out, we will do everything possible to ensure that the rules of the game will be enforced so that you are protected from unnecessary violence."

Taking a breath, he said, "What do you think, Keith? I know this is out of the clear blue and you have every right to feel blindsided, but…we want you to consider our request."

I didn't know what to think, it was scary to consider going out for football to play and practice with Duke and the many rednecks on the Demons football team and then I couldn't help think of the reception I'd get on football fields in small North Florida towns like Monticello. But an overriding thought trumped everything: I thought I'd be good, and I wanted to show off my skills-to myself, my family, White folk and everybody else, especially Black girls. I had thought about playing football before because football was king in the FAMU community-Rattler football games at the lavish Bragg stadium were the center of social life in the community and I had never missed attending home games. In contrast, basketball, the next most popular sport on FAMU's campus, was played and poorly-attended, in a decrepit field house.

"Mr. Bishop, I'll talk to my dad and get back to you tomorrow morning with my answer," I said.

So, I knew, even as I headed toward French class, what my answer would be-I was going to be a football player. I knew my dad and my mom would be all for it, if it was something I wanted. And, for some reason I wanted it.

After French Class, I confided in Tim as we walked down the bustling hallway about my visit with Principal Bishop. Listening to my recounting of the visit, his broad face assumed a contemplative expression. Though a smile tentatively lifted the corners of his mouth, his eyes were distinctly humorless. With his lumbering walk, slightly stooped shoulders, and only a hint of a waist, Tim did not appear to be the second team All-State defensive back (as a sophomore) that he was. Despite his open friendship with Mahlon and me, Duke and his Kluxxer crew had only infrequently harassed him as a "Nigger Lover" perhaps because of his football prowess, but more likely because his father taught mathematics on the Florida High faculty.

"Keith, I know you can help us, but there is a core of guys on the team-those following Duke-who are very much against your coming out," said Tim. "I don't know if Bishop told you this, but last week the whole team met with Coach Rose right after practice just to discuss your joining the team, and after the meeting, there was a vote. It was close, something like 24 to 19 and I don't think the vote would have been for you had it not been by secret ballot and if Coach Rose hadn't made a plea on your behalf. And he even stated at the beginning that he was against integration. But I think he said it was a 'necessary evil' that we have to live with and that you were a good boy who could help the team."

As we walked toward the lunchroom and I listened to Tim, the euphoric feeling I'd had that I was so special began to dissipate; and it was slowly replaced by an unrelenting fear about what I was getting myself into.

"Even with Coach Rose kind of speaking out for me," I said, "I'm still surprised a majority of the team favored my coming out, especially two games into the season."

Tim responded, "There were a number of players like Randy Driggs and Jim Shelfer who I don't think voted for you to join the team but only because they were influenced by Duke who was really mad just before the vote and said that "if any Nigger joined the team, he would quit!" After the vote, Coach Rose called Duke into his office. They were still behind that closed door when I left.

As Tim and I approached the cafeteria, we were met by Tim's girlfriend Lynn. She was a pretty girl with thick-lashed eyes and a great figure, although with her hair in a tightly drawn bun and loose-fitting clothes, she did not appear to care about competing with other female students in the glamour department. Tim had told me that her father, an attorney, was not a fan of civil rights. I noticed, nevertheless, that when she spoke to us, she did so openly and warmly. A year behind Tim and me, she too was scholarly and her and Tim's relationship was perfectly matched-neither apparently cared about being "in."

After she spoke to me, she and Tim, who, as usual seemed like a love-sick puppy in her presence, walked off toward the library where they almost always spent their lunch periods. I mindlessly watched them walk away, digesting Tim's earlier comments and did not notice Mahlon approach and stand at my side. He said, eyes twinkling, "Who you looking at so hard, good brother? If it's that White girl, you risking a lynching; and if it's Tim, I'm not going to hang around you anymore."

I laughed and we headed toward the cafeteria. I told Mahlon about my meeting with Bishop and my tentative decision to go out for the football team. He said that it was "cool" for me to go out and that he knew I would "raise hell." But his words of encouragement did not mask the disappearance of the recent twinkle from his eyes which had been replaced by a serious cast which seemed to reflect his real doubts about my sanity. I wondered why my decision seemed to precipitate solemnity in my friends, but as I thought about how bad it was being the only Black person on basketball courts in North Florida, I couldn't rid myself of the thought that it would have to be infinitely worse on football fields where violent hitting was the norm.

My subsequent discussions with my parents were anti-climactic. My dad beamed with the thought of my playing football. He reminded me that he'd played in high school and with apparent tongue in cheek had recalled playing center for his high school team and on one occasion beating down a rival, allegedly a 300-pound nose tackle, to the extent that the nose tackle was crying at game's end.

After my mom lamented that she didn't want me to get hurt, upon hearing that I really wanted to go out, she gave me her blessing to do so if that was what I wanted. It was a done deal: the next day I would be integrating the Florida High football team.

Katrina, my younger sister by eight years' was all for the idea of m playing football. "I know my big brother will be a star. I'm not worried about that at all." Katrina's support was inspirational. She had Cerebral Palsy since birth which caused her to have to walk with braces and crutches. Mentally, she was sharp as a tack with a wicked sense of humor. She never let the unfairness of her getting CP at birth (before she'd had a chance to sin or to praise God's glory) remove the joy from her life. Despite the obstacles confronting her, she was a very devout Christian and a great, supportive sister.

The next day at 2:30 p.m., I knocked on the closed office door where Coach Dick Rose of the University of Alabama Class of 1941 ran an operation built on a state-wide renown for turning out highly competitive Class B football teams.

"It's open," boomed Coach Rose in his usual hoarse voice. The small windowless office had a singular motif-high school football. A large Demons football schedule topped a calendar from Garcia's Restaurant, a Cuban restaurant downtown to which Black diners were not yet welcome, owned and operated by the parents of the Garcia brothers, reputedly the two best JV players. Under the calendar was a bookshelf filled with books of the "winning high school football" genre.

Coach Rose walked from behind his neat little desk, reached out a meat hook of a hand which I shook while trying not to wince upon receiving the kind of handshake one would expect from a man whose job as he saw it-and as he told all of his PE classes-was to mold boys into Kamakazi hitters on the football field. He bellowed, "Keith, my boy, I guess Bishop spoke to you about joining the Demon football family. One thing I can say about Bishop is that for a Yankee, he sho' loves his football. I'm tickled to death that you decided to come out. I think you could be our own Bob Hayes with all that speed you have."

I had nothing to respond to the Bob Hayes reference, but it didn't matter. Coach Rose's verbosity often didn't allow for dialogue. I noticed the five team pictures adorning the wall behind him; team portraits of old Demon state championship teams dated '55, '57, '59, '60 and '62. I figured that the four-year drought from the last championship to the present coupled with this year's 0-2 start had caused "good-ole boy" Dick Rose to give in to that "necessary evil."

"Keith, I know you can throw the hell out of the ball, but my son Al is our quarterback and I see you catching a bunch of bombs from him-that sound good? I honestly believe with you to throw deep to, he would start getting some interest from the big schools-maybe even from my old school Bama. Roll Tide!"

When I failed to respond, he stopped smiling and leaned closer, looking me in the eyes. "We like to think of Florida High football as one big family, and now you're going to be a member of this family-its first Colored member. I have to be honest with you, a number of players don't feel that anybody should be able to step right on to the varsity team who didn't participate in spring drills-especially two games into the season. It has nothing to do with the fact that you're Colored. We feel it's an honor for any young man to play on the Demon football team, an honor that has to be earned. So what we're going to do is fit you up with pads and start you out with the junior varsity. So Coach Childs will be waiting for you over on South field to begin practice today. We're going to start you off as a tailback/flanker, 'cause with your speed, you should be the "Black lighting" of this Demon team."

Coach Rose's smile displayed tobacco-stained teeth. Eyes twinkling, his mouth continued to flow, "Who knows, Keith?" he said, while turning his seat and pointing to the pictures of championship pictures, "maybe this year or next, you'll be included in one of those pictures." Chuckling, he kept going, "You'd sho' nuff be a standout in one of those pictures, like a lump of coal in a snow drift."

Perhaps noting my strained effort to smile at his last witticism, the craggy lines of his face instantaneously changed from one of all out levity, to one of a seriously concerned adult. "Keith, I've always got along good with your people. When I was growing up in Walnut Grove Alabama-that's 47 miles south of Birmingham-some of my best friends as a young boy was Colored; why Lester Jenkins and me used to fish all the time down at the creek and 'ole' Lester was, and probably still is, black as the ace of spades. Another thing you should know, Keith, me and the Missus have always had Colored maids; the one we got now we've had for nine years." He continued, "You might know her-Zelma Brown?"

I shook my head.

"I'm telling you Zelma is like family-I mean almost like a momma to Ben and Bubba." Pausing momentarily as if in search of a verbal coup de grace, he continued, "Every Christmas we always send her and her husband James, who works down at St. Joe pulp mill, a good bottle of gin."

"That's nice," I said quietly trying not to sound as disgusted as I was.

"Okay, Keith, my boy, let's go get you fitted up in pads." He stood up and came around his desk. He playfully threw his right arm around my neck, opened his office door and with an arm still around my neck like I was his best buddy, we left his office and headed down the hall to the equipment room.

Little more than halfway down the hallway, we approached the door-less entrance to the varsity locker room on the left. I was familiar with it because during basketball season, I was assigned to one of its extra large lockers. Given the presence of Duke and his boys dressing and undressing within its cramped domain, I never even looked toward it during football season. With his arm still loosely around my neck, Coach Rose and I passed the doorway. I apprehensively looked in. Confirming my fears, I saw Duke looking like a polar bear wearing only a jock strap and a number of other players in varying stages of undress. No sooner had we passed the doorway when a chorus of rebel yells and pig calls echoed out of the small locker room.

"Dark meat for supper today, my boys." The unmistakable shrill voice of the Duke thundered above all others.

Coach Rose, who had been rambling on about how my speed would help our offense in general and Ben's passing stats in particular stopped his monologue upon hearing the players' raucous reaction but kept his eyes straight ahead. I looked over my left shoulder and saw that Duke, Mallory and two other players had exited the locker room and were standing in the hallway. Seeing my glance, Duke's ear to ear smile vanished and he sneered, "I can't wait to get some dark meat today, boy."

Instinctively looking to Coach Rose to reprimand his players, I saw that his sun-reddened face had unbelievably reddened more. And to my dismay, he said nothing to his players, although it was telling how quickly he had removed his arm from around my neck.

I found the outbursts of Duke and the others to be especially disturbing because while I had been called every name the creative White Southern mind could come up with, there had never on those occasions been a school authority figure present. Rather, in the past, none of the vocal bigots had ever chanced manifesting their hatred for the students of color in the presence of teachers or coaches-until today. Yet Coach Rose had said nothing to chastise my tormentors, nor had he said anything in support of my rattled psyche. I couldn't help thinking that I would not do well in the business of football without the support, indeed, the protection of, the coaching staff.

In the equipment room, Coach Rose, for the purpose of impressing upon me the level of hitting I should expect as a Demon football player, tossed me a helmet that had once been maroon, but was scarred with White pock marks. At his behest, I tried it on. It smelled of sweat and something else that I concluded was Brylcream. Never having worn a helmet before, I felt boxed in, as if my peripheral vision had been cut in half.

Slapping me lightly on the helmet, Coach Rose once again in a jovial vein chuckled. "You look mean already."

Seamlessly slipping back into his "tough coach persona" he leaned closer to me. "Keith, I want you to be a crazed hitter-that's the only way to gain their respect. I want you to be a mean son-of- a-bitch. I want you to knock some more of that maroon paint off that helmet."

I made no effort to look him in his eyes that were trying fixate on mine. It was all so ludicrous; here he was asking me to go out on the field and hit people, when it had been made crystal clear not ten minutes earlier that most of the players I would face, including my teammates, were looking forward with relish to me being the hittee.

As I sat there wearing the stupid, foul-smelling helmet, I had to come to grips with the fact that no one was forcing me to play football. I was volunteering to play football for Florida High-a football team that I had previously cared for so little that, for my first two years at FHS, I had never gone to a game. But I thought I'd be seriously good at the game. It was solely because of that ego-driven belief that I didn't bolt out of that equipment room yelling over my shoulder where Coach Rose could place my bundle of equipment.

After giving me all the gear I'd need, he said, "Okay, Keith, my boy, take your gear over to locker 41." He handed me the combination tag. "It's over where the JV players dress," he continued. "Don't worry, though, 'cause you'll soon be practicing with the big boys. So today, report to Coach Childs over at the South Field."

I picked up my equipment and headed out of the equipment room in which Coach Rose remained, so I steeled myself for the approaching confrontation with my new teammates. As anticipated, Duke and a couple of others were standing just in the hallway at the entrance to the varsity locker room.

Seeing me walking toward them, Duke shouted, "Here he comes. Hey Garland, here comes your nigger friend. Look at him carrying his pads like some 'nigger' washerwoman. Boy, we can't wait to get a chance to knock yo' ass out."

More players appeared in the entrance way, all seeming to want a glance at the novelty-a Black boy crazy enough to come out by himself for their football team. As I got closer, a player standing next to Duke, pointed his finger at me and said, "Boy your ass is in serious trouble." Hate distorted his face.

As I drew a couple of feet closer to my welcoming committee, I saw that Coach Jobie Childs, all 5'8 of him, was coming down the far-end of the hallway. Since the players were concentrating on me they were oblivious to his approach. So from different directions, Coach Childs and I intersected with the players at the entrance to the varsity locker room just as Duke was yelling, "A cigar? No, a Niggar." In response to Mallory having yelled, "I smell a 'Gar.'"

Coach Childs jumped in Duke's face and it was heartening for me to see Duke take a step back with a look of surprise across his broad face. The players around Duke collectively took a step backward as Coach Childs flew into them.

"What's wrong with you boys?" he bellowed, with a big voice that belied the relatively small body from which it emanated.

I gingerly stepped pass Coach Childs' back and continued up the hallway without looking back at the on-going confrontation. As I walked away, I heard Coach Childs' voice, "There is no way we're gonna tolerate this sort of thing. Y'all get back in that locker room and get dressed. After practice, Duke, I want you and your five mob members with the big mouths to meet me at South field after your practice for a few extra wind sprints. Just tell Coach Rose that y'all are running them as a favor to me."

Stealing a glance over my shoulder, I saw little Coach Childs pushing the mammoth Duke and his buddies into the locker room. I smiled despite my circumstances-at least one coach had my back.

As I approached the junior varsity locker room, I knew there would be a reaction though I didn't anticipate epithets as delivered by my varsity teammates. As expected, the playful voices I heard upon my initial entrance drew silent. It felt in the silence like everyone's eyes were on me as I sat down in front of locker 41. After opening my locker, I started to try to unravel and make sense of the alien pads and gear. To my dismay, I saw that there were no pads in my football pants; so I decided to try to figure out where my football pants' pads went before I tried to determine if it made a difference which way I put my shoulder pads on.

"So, what position you going out for?"

I looked around to see Martin Garcia, looking as hostile as he could with a baby face that made him look for the world like Lucy's Little Ricky. He was standing in front of his brother and two other JV players, clearly the spokesman for the group.

"Coach Rose said I'd be playing halfback," I replied.

Frowning, it was evident that he'd been expecting and dreading hearing what I'd told him. He glanced back at his crew as if to draw courage from their presence.

"Well," he sneered, "I've been the first team right halfback, and my brother Vincent has played left halfback." A slightly taller version of Martin stepped forward at the mention of his name. Martin continued, "And it doesn't seem right for you to be allowed to come out a week before our first game and get handed the positions we've work for."

Not liking that they were standing over me as I sat on the bench, I stood up.

"Look," I said, staring into Martin's jet-black eyes, "I'm not going out to take anybody's position. I..." As I paused to try to articulate why I was going out, Coach Childs, who was earning a reputation for getting me out of tight places, rounded the corner and walked over. Coach Childs was young-three years out of Florida State where he'd joined the team as a walk-on, and had progressed to the starting free safety position despite his slender 5'9" built.

In his high-pitched, nasal voice he stated, "Well, I'm glad that some of you JV boys have already introduced y'all selves to our newest team member."

I had to guess Coach Childs was being sarcastic since I'm sure Ray Charles could have seen that the intent of my JV welcoming committee had not been based in cordiality.

"I guess that Martin's just checking up on some of the competition," Coach Childs said. "You boys better hurry up and get dressed, cause if you're late for practice, that's gonna be grounds for you to volunteer to run extra wind sprints."

Players made a mad rush to their lockers and started hurriedly getting dressed. I couldn't help wondering if Coach Childs threatened his wife with wind sprints when he got mad at her.

Coach Childs stepped over to me and extended his hand which I shook. "Nice meeting you," he said. His twinkling brown eyes seemed to contain genuine warmth. "I hear you were drafted by none other than Principal Bishop himself."

"I guess you could say that," I mumbled, shrugging my shoulders.

"I also hear you've never played organized football before," he continued. "I hope you can bear with me as I introduce you to this fine game. But I've got to let you know up front that I've never coached before, although I can promise you I will do my damnedest to teach you and your teammates the right way to play this game."

I sat down on the bench. "Coach I don't even know how to put my pads together."

I heard a muffled snicker from my immediate left where an overweight player whose stomach was protruding over the top of his pants was awkwardly trying to dress at the locker two down from mine without getting too close.

Coach Childs' eyes darted in the snickerer's direction and he snapped, "What's so funny, Rexford?"

"Nothing at all coach," Rexford said obsequiously as he grabbed his helmet and waddled out the door to the practice fields.

"Well, Keith, my boy," Coach Childs said, "I can give you a little help with that."

Sitting next to me he deftly inserted the pads into place.

"Don't worry, it's a simple process. It has to be because football players as a group aren't real bright," he said chuckling. Finishing quickly, he stood up, "Any other questions?"

I shook my head. He turned to leave and turned abruptly back around and sat down. The area by that time had cleared out. In an almost hushed tone, he stated, "Keith, we're gonna have to bring you on kind of fast. Coach Rose has told me that as soon as I think you're ready, he wants you over with the varsity." He paused and continued, "This is not going to be the easiest thing you've ever done, Keith, but if you have just half the talent that I've heard you have and if you work yo' tail off, I guarantee you'll get everybody's respect."

Squirming a bit, he softly continued, "I was born and raised in this town, I went to Leon. The only real dealings I had with your people were a little bit adver-adversarial if I'm pronouncing that right and I ain't real proud of some of them," he said. "Like when I was at Leon, me and some of my friends would throw rocks at the Colored kids walking past Leon to the Colored school about two miles away. I must admit we called them names, but God knows I didn't hate them. It was just the way things were back then.

Coach Childs continued, "But I must tell you, I got a double dose of respect for your people on and off the athletic field my senior year at FSU when Houston brought in that little scatback, Warren Murphy, the first Colored guy we'd ever played against. Even though he wasn't any bigger than me, he had to have been one tough son-of-a-gun because we did our best to intimidate him. We would threaten that we were going to hurt him, we piled on him when he was down, we hit him late a couple of times and we called him names, but he just smiled and single-handedly destroyed us. He blew past me so many times, I swear for a lot of the game, I couldn't tell what race he was. He could have been Irish. As the game ended, I had developed a boatload of respect for Murphy. He had certainly beat us with his physical skills, but more than that, at least to me, he never lost his cool in the face of our ignorance. He almost had a serenity about him no matter how much me and my teammates acted the fool. I found myself regretting that I had been a part of our efforts to demean him; I couldn't help but wonder how I would have acted if I had been in his situation as the only White boy playing against an all-Colored team.

"So I made up my mind and went over to their locker room and waited as the Houston players came out. Warren came out alone, he was the only Colored guy on the team. I walked up to him and introduced myself. He was real outgoing; we talked about the game and he didn't appear to hold it against me that I had called him out his name early in the game. We talked a while and I found that we got along well. Before I knew it, I asked him to come have dinner at my Mother's house. I'll tell you the initial shock of me walking in the front door of her house with a Colored boy almost made her faint. But I must tell you, I was so proud of the old girl, she had made her specialty-chicken and dumplings-and was as nice to him as she could be, especially since he was the first Colored man in her house. And he really charmed her to death. He said that, like her, his mother was a good cook. Flashing a wicked smile, he'd even told her that he didn't know that White people could cook so well.

"After dinner, my mother hugged Warren good bye and I took him back to the hotel where his team was staying. Back at my mom's, she and I had a long talk about people in general that there were decent people of all races. She and I agreed that my dad was probably spinning like a top in his grave, but she had seen for the first time up close and personal how wrong it was to prejudge people because of skin color so she and I were really changed by the whole thing. And the fact that some of my teammates started jokingly calling me Martin Luther for a while, or anything else changed the new feelings that I developed on the day of the Houston game."

As if pricked by a pin, Coach Childs jumped up and sheepishly apologized. "Keith, I'm sorry, I got carried away-but I had to get this off my chest," Coach Childs said. "Don't get me wrong though, I don't plan on joining any civil rights marches, but I hope my sharing that story with you can somehow build a bridge of trust between us. Just know that you can talk to me about your problems. OK, Keith?"

"Yes, Coach," I responded.

He quickly glanced at his watch and started toward the hallway. Looking back over his shoulder, he added, "Since I have no excuse for being late, I guess I'll be running extra wind sprints after practice."

After Coach Childs left, I found myself digesting his epiphany. I could not stop wondering what his position would have been on race relations if Murphy had been an easily intimidated, average player. Metaphorically, might he be still throwing rocks and yelling ugly names? I couldn't help wondering, but I still liked Coach Childs.

My first day of football practice was anticlimactic. I mostly watched, practiced the right way to accept handoffs, blocked tackling dummies, did calisthenics and, of course, wind sprints. As I watched my JV teammates, I could see even with no organized football in my background that a lot of them were not very skilled.

The most interesting of the tackling drills was saved for last and was called the "nut cracker." In it, two tackling dummies were placed five yards apart. A defensive player took position between the dummies, the ball was handed to a back who ran between the dummies and tried to make as many yards as he could against the wishes of the defensive player. This drill was the classic manhood check and except for Martin Garcia bowling over a bigger defensive player (I had to smile to see it had been Rexford), most of the time the defensive player got the best of the contact, often knocking the running back backward. It was evident that this drill was a morale-booster during practice and players circled enthusiastically around the drill. Frequent shouts went up from players and coaches imploring the defensive players to "bow" their necks. The drill was a toughness gauge and I knew players would watch closely my participation to evaluate my heart. I was wondering what I'd show them.

The next day, the first thing I noticed were the dozen or so spectators who'd come to watch the FHS JV practice. Remembering the number of curious spectators at my first junior high basketball practice, I realized that I had an apparent talent for increasing interest in even the most obscure FHS sports teams. Three of the spectators wore letterman jackets indicating that they had played football and had graduated the year before. Unless I was projecting-and I knew I wasn't-- they seemed to be glaring exclusively at me. During the long practice, I learned about running plays, especially the hole to hit as assigned by the play called, and other fundamentals.

Coach Childs' high-pitched voice rang out, "Okay men, let's get together and crack some nuts."

The players and the spectators enthusiastically moved closer to the two almost ceremoniously placed dummies.

Coach Childs called out, "Gimme Martin Garcia carrying the ball and DeForest on defense."

"Bow your neck, DeForest, and stick him," one of the letter-jacketed graduates yelled. I noticed it was the oldest of the three Black-folks hating Peece brothers-Bill. After handing the ball to Martin, DeForest, a 6' 185-pound linebacker, met him head-on but couched lower with his knees churning. Martin fell backward-an undeniable win for the defense.

"Martin step out, Keith step in and carry the ball," Coach Childs yelled.

My chest tightened up. I hadn't expected to be put on the spot so quickly and against the best defensive player on the team.

"Show that boy who's boss DeForest," the Love brother

yelled.

My teammates were all telling him to, "Stick him" and to "Bow his neck." It was me against the world and I couldn't stop a thought from instantaneously crossing my mind: don't be a punk and let Black folks down deliver a blow. Having watched the A&M Rattlers practice throughout my childhood, I had heard Rattler Backfield Coach, Bob Mungen, my neighbor, tell his running backs to always try to make the tackler get the worse of the contact by staying low and running hard.

On the second "hut," I accepted the ball from Coach Childs properly-left arm up and bent horizontally at the elbow. I immediately switched it so that I carried it in the crook of my left arm which freed my right arm. Just prior to impact with the well-positioned DeForest I bent myself so that I was running low thereby providing a target of mostly helmet, shoulder pads, and knees. I threw my right forearm at the front of his helmet as we made a hard jarring contact. At that very moment, I instinctively made a spin move off my left foot. DeForest fell back and almost lost grip of me as I spun, and tackled me by holding on to my foot from behind. I'd gained eight yards.

"Way to run, Keith!" Coach Childs all but squealed. "Where in the world did you learn to run like that?"

I was beaming, the spin move had been all instinct, my hard running had been a by- product of my refusal, on the football field, to allow myself to be humiliated in front of White folks. I knew I wasn't a tough guy, but there was no reason my teammates had to know that. I had a similar positive result on the second time I participated in the nut cracker and looked forward to participating in the short scrimmage we were to have at the end of our practice day.

During the scrimmage, I ran the ball five times. The first three times, I gained a grand total of three yards. On those runs, by the time I hit the assigned holes, there were none there. After those ineffective efforts, Coach Childs called me aside. "Keith, when you hit a hole you look like you're starting to run a 440 and you're gliding to it. You got to change that mindset, Son. Hit the assigned hole like you're running a 10 yard dash, in other words as fast as you can."

Employing Coach Childs' suggestion, I was almost past the quarterback before receiving the handoff on my fourth carry and found myself at the side of the linebacker who grabbed my leg and pulled me down after I'd gained six yards. My fifth and final run found me hitting the hole so fast, the linebacker was left behind. I ran until I crossed the goal line. The touchdown was special, and I couldn't help expecting many more-I'd made the right decision going out for football. I quickly learned that there was no consensus that I'd be good.

After practice, walking toward our locker room, lost in my own positive thoughts, I heard in little more than a whisper, "Nigger, don't think you're so good 'cause you ran over these little boys. Duke and the varsity got something for your Black ass when you get up there with the big boys."

I looked over and saw the letter jacket of the older Love brother brush past me. He had discreetly spoken to me as he'd walked by. It was just enough to totally dissipate my euphoria at how good I thought I'd be and it let me know that doing well in a JV scrimmage didn't mean I had arrived but that the journey had just started.

Two days later on a Thursday evening, the Florida High JV football team lined up to play the Perry High Baby Hornets. As we performed our calisthenics, I found myself staring at the green and white clad boys from Perry. I had already tried to convince myself that the junior varsity from Perry, Florida could not be the bunch of maniacal head hunters Coach Childs had described. But then no such attempts to minimize the threat of the thoroughly White boys from rural Perry outweighed my dad's ill-advised observation that the last lynching in the state had occurred in Perry in the mid-1950s.

We received the opening kickoff which Vincent Garcia took twelve yards to the thirty-one yard line. After a sweep right, a sweep left, and a dive right-all by Martina-total of seven yards had been made. The Perry boys did seem to hit hard; their players swarmed to the ball carrier, each one trying to get a piece of the action. If the tackle had been made, they piled on. They seemed to be a mean bunch, led by a particularly nasty linebacker, number 47, who tackled hard-driving players into the ground often after the play had been whistled dead. He was good-sized and seemed to be enthusiastically in on every tackle.

By second quarter, the Baby Demons were on the short side of a 7-0 score. We were doing nothing offensively. Our running game was nonexistent. Martin was not only failing to make any positive yardage, he was getting punished by hard tackles made worse because he ran in too upright a manner.

Early in the second quarter, Martin accepted a handoff and crumbled upon a hard tackle by "47" as the linebacker drove him into the ground. Martin got up slowly and as he walked stiff-legged back to the huddle, Coach Childs called out, "Keith, get in there for Martin."

Martin seemed relieved to see me at the huddle, and he ran toward our sideline faster than he'd run all night. When we broke the huddle and I lined up in the backfield, I saw that "47" was bouncing up and down and talking incessantly at me.

"We gonna get you boy!" he said. "I'm gon' personally knock your ass out."

My first play was a sweep right. I ran crouched down right behind my offensive linemen. "47" was right where he should have been and made a jarring tackle despite my efforts to fake him at the point of impact.

"That jiggaboo shit ain't working out here, boy," he barked.

While I couldn't argue the point, I noticed that I'd gained 5 yards-our longest run of the night. The next play was a dive right-a straight-ahead run. I resolved to hit the assigned hole as quick as I could. When the ball was snapped, I shot out of my stance, accepted the ball, and found myself-for a split second-face to face with "47." He crouched in perfect form to make the tackle, I went at him hard but under control. He lurched forward, making solid impact with my right shin, but just as I was spinning around on my left leg as I'd done in the first nut cracker drill. Coming out of the spin, fighting frantically to regain my balance, I could see a lonely expanse of field with the goal post in the horizon.

A defensive back closing in on my right presented little problem; I was gone. I almost laughed out loud as I, despite myself, pranced the last ten yards into the end zone. As I headed to our sideline, I saw the blood trickling down my right shin which had been split to the "white meat." A couple of my teammates hit me on the shoulder pads and told me, "Nice run."

Coach Childs hugged me and beamed. "Keith, you're making me one hell of a coach already."

The rest of the game had been my showcase. I ran for another touchdown, caught an underthrown touchdown pass, and brought a punt back 40 yards before stepping out of bounds to avoid getting creamed on the sideline. I knew that wasn't exactly bowing my neck, but I felt self-preservation trumped feigned toughness.

After my last run, I saw that I was being substituted for. In turning to run to our bench, I closely passed "47."

Uncharacteristically cocky, I said to him as I passed, "I guess the jiggaboo shit worked alright."

Coach Rose

Coach Rose was almost giddy after seeing Keith play. He knew about what he could add to the varsity offense and Ben's passing stats.

He began walking across the field in search of the Perry varsity football coach, Hawk Benson, a close friend and rival through the years. He knew Hawk's interest in the future of his varsity team necessitated his presence at the JV game.

The Perry JV players were huddled at the end of the bench around their young coach who was screaming at them that they had not played hard enough for all four quarters.

Perry fans, largely in time-worn farming or truck driving attire, swarmed the area, their attitude surly.

"That nigger boy was the difference. Next thing you know, they gonna name this school Martin Luther King," a red-faced man in a cap with *Perry Trucking* on its crown said to another red-faced man who nodded in total agreement.

Coach Rose saw Coach Benson talking to a man and a woman. As he walked in their direction, the two red-faced men, noting the Florida High Coaching Staff on Coach Rose's golf shirt inquired, "Y'all went out and found yourselves a live one, huh Coach?"

Eyes straight ahead, Coach Rose kept walking-he refused to acknowledge them.

When he got over to where Coach Benson was holding court, Benson stopped his conversation with the couple to whom he'd been speaking and greeted him warmly. "Dick, you ole' swamp dog, how're you doing?"

"I'm doing okay, Hawk, since it's almost a month before you bring that outstanding varsity team of yours up here."

Coach Benson introduced the couple to whom he had been

talking as the parents of "that stud, number 47." They both smiled, but the woman's eyes were fiercely piercing.

"Coach," she started, her voice was surprisingly feminine but was possessed of a highly-evident edge, "that Colored boy shouldn't have been out there. I'm told he's a junior, he should be on your varsity-he ruined a damn good team of JV players."

"Ma'am, he is a junior, but he just came out for football last week," Coach Rose said. "He'll be moving up shortly. By the way, y'all got at least three or four juniors on this JV team and I happen to know that your son is a 17-year-old sophomore."

"That's right," Coach Benson interjected. "Mrs. White, you know we start a half-dozen juniors on this JV team. And if that Colored boy, by his little 160-pound self, demoralized this team, well, shame on us."

"It's just not right," she lamented. "That Colored boy just doesn't belong out there with White boys. Come on, Jesse, let's go see how little Jess is doing." She grabbed the arm of her sad-sack husband and ushered him away from the coaches.

"Dick, that Colored boy looks like he can sho' nuff improve your coaching skills; why you wasting your time with him on JV?"

"Hell, Coach," Coach Rose responded, "I had a hard time getting a lot of my players to accept him coming out at all this year. I mean, a lot of my boys don't want a Colored boy on the team period. It's halfway into the season." He and Benson walked slowly across the football field talking earnestly.

"I couldn't just bring him up and put him on Varsity," Coach Rose continued. "I just don't know, Andy…hell, I ain't in favor of integration, but dammit integration is here. We only got five or six here now, but more are coming. That Colored boy is fast and elusive as a greased pig, you saw it, and my team is slow. I can use his speed."

"You know, Dick, I don't know if I would play him unless I had to, but I understand," Benson said. "Perry ain't ready for that race-mixing shit, though some of the local Colored folks are starting to make demands. But we just ain't ready for them Black boys to be leering after our girls, Dick.

"That Colored boy really destroyed my junior varsity. We thought we were good. I don't know if you should bring him down to Perry next week," Hawk said. "I mean, he would catch hell down there even if folks hadn't seen him this week, but anticipating y'all bringing in a super-star Nigra down there they'll be in a frenzy. I'll call you, Dick to be sure."

They stopped at mid field, Benson trying to go back toward the still-milling crowd of Perry supporters.

"I better get back to my mob, Dick," Hawk said. "Take care of yourself and if you get to any more fast Black boys, we gonna have to drop you all from the schedule." He turned and walked toward the crowd.

As he turned to walk back to the home side of the field, he knew that Benson's last statement was not a throw-away line.

> "The boy can play and he's fast, and Ben throws deep
> well, Coach Rose thought. He can help my team, he
> can help Ben. I've done right."

Someone from the Perry crowd yelled something that he heard loud and clear. Coach Rose flushed and was instantly overcome with anger. He had fought plenty of times as a young boy with less provocation. But he did not look back and he did not break stride as echoes of what was yelled resounded in his mind, "Nigger Lover."

On Wednesday before practice for the second Perry JV game on Friday night, Coach Childs-with embarrassed eyes-told me that the Perry coach had strongly suggested that I not accompany the junior Demons to Perry because the town folks were still seething that "a Colored boy" had contributed greatly to the defeat of their beloved little "rednecks."

Coach Childs had been so apologetic-as if Perry's ignorance was his fault-even though I tried to tell him that I didn't mind. I didn't. I would have been scared to death going to Perry on Friday night all by my lonesome Black self.

I knew immediately what I was going to be doing when my teammates were playing Perry; I was going to go to the movies up on FAMU's campus, and then I was going to the after-game dance following FAMU High's game against crosstown rival Lincoln High. I wanted to dance slow with a nice-looking girl who was Black like me.

Mahlon, I knew, would not be going with me. He had gone with Celeste's family to their beach property for the weekend. He had told me how Celeste's mother was one of those liberal types of moms, unusual in our community, who believed that her teenage daughter was grown just because that daughter was built like a grown woman. So even on family outings, Mahlon and Celeste were given ample opportunities to be alone. And Mahlon just loved to tell me about her receptive attitude.

On Friday night, I put on an outfit that was considered in my mind as "clean" even though it screamed "White Boy." I wore a madras Gant shirt, solid pants, and burgundy loafers. That was how I liked to dress-preppy-that was me. The Friday night movies on FAMU's campus was part of my friends' regular social agenda. The movies downtown had begrudgingly started to admit Black folks, but it was not really conducive to enjoying a flick when you were being called Nigger or having popcorn or sodas thrown at you.

In delicious contrast, at FAMU's Friday night movies, you could have fun. The campus movies were not what you'd call "first-run," but if you hadn't seen them, they were "first-run" to you. The only potential problem you might run into as a high school guy in an arena with college boys was that you were susceptible to getting bullied. It didn't happen that much, but if you were taking or, more likely, meeting a girl there, the college guys would totally disrespect you by beckoning her or boldly approaching her. There wasn't much a high school guy could do short of calling out the disrespecting college guy and even fighting him. For me, fighting a college boy was not high on my "to do" list.

Fortunately, when meeting me at the movies Bennetta, my former girlfriend of one year, who was a certified cutie paid the beseeching college boys no attention and stayed close to me. She honestly seemed to dislike the attention from the leering college boys.

But this Friday night, I did not have Bennetta to proudly squire around. She had blatantly dumped me earlier that summer at a Jack and Jill Regional Annual Convention in Mobile for an Iranian-looking "pretty boy" from Pensacola. The Jack and Jill club was a national organization which was started for upper class people of color usually of the lighter hew (though I, as recently-elected President of our teen chapter, was among a growing number of brown-skinned members). Each year, the organization scheduled for

80

its members social events, educationally enlightening visits to museums, plays, symphonic concerts international teas and occasionally, community projects. The regional annual conventions were three-day meetings of regional city chapters of J&J that convened in different cities mostly to provide more direct opportunities for teen members to meet and greet one another. In Mobile-even though she was supposedly, at the time, my girlfriend-Bennetta had humiliated me. I had been humiliated because all my friends knew that I had been "kicked to the curb." After the regional, the Pensacola guy drove two hours each way to visit her almost every other weekend.

So with no Bennetta, I was going to the movies alone not knowing if any of my crowd would be there. I hadn't really wanted to go to the game because, well, while everybody there would have been Black like me or some colorful variation, I still did not fit in there. I blended, but I didn't belong. I had left FAMU High and all my friends there to "cross the street" to the White school-in essence, saying that the Black school, the Black teachers, and the Black students were not good enough for me. I felt like, at the game, and for that matter the dance, I would not have been welcomed.

I remembered the last FAMU High game I'd gone to last year. Clair Warner, a former classmate of mine, had asked in front of several students why-if FAMU High wasn't good enough for me to attend-I would want to go to a football game there. I didn't answer her, but I knew the reason I came back to the FAMU High dances was because there were lots of Black girls there and I did not have to take furtive peeks at them.

As I walked into the cafeteria where the dance was being held, I heard that the Baby Rattlers had beaten Lincoln in a nail-biter: 13-7. I could not have cared less. My mind was focused on a slow drag; in fact I was determined to become-oh my mother would have been so hurt-a serial slow dragger.

The lights were probably a little lower than the parents of a daughter would have wanted, but I thought the atmosphere was perfect. The girls and boys for the most part sat on opposite sides of the dance floor-watching each other without really seeming to be so engaged.

I guess like any other high school, there were cliques at FAMU High. The snob group included the children of the professors and administrators along with the kids of the few doctors and lawyers in town-essentially the Jack and Jill crowd. Frequently, though not all the time-certainly I, as President of the Tallahassee teen chapter was among the exceptions-these kids tended to be light-skinned.

Then there were the kids whose parents worked in staff positions. They could hang with the preppy faction or the city kids whose parents were unaffiliated with FAMU, although if they were "light" and attractive enough, they were guaranteed acceptance by the preppy kids.

I was basically alone that night. The guys in the prep crowd were not that big on FAMU High after-game dances. I saw a former classmate, the always colorfully dressed Ralph Coleman talking to another former classmate, the short, squat LeNard Gary. I walked over, unsure of the reception I'd get. Ralph lived down the street from me and had always been somebody I kind of looked up to; Mahlon had basically followed him as a clique-leader in grades fourth and fifth. Ralph was a year older than we were because he had repeated the second or third grade. Probably as a result, Ralph was better at sports than the rest of us.

I was happy to see Ralph smile when I approached. "Well if it's not a Florida High Demon. What brings you over on this side of the tracks, my man?"

"What's up," I said. "I just went to the movies on campus and thought I'd stop in to see if I could learn some new dance steps watching you, good brother." LeNard watched non-committedly.

Ralph smiled broader. "Boy, you just want to get next to some of these fine sisters over here," he said. "You ain't fooling nobody. You can't even look at none of them White girls over there, now can you?"

"Not 'less I want to be hanging from some tree," I joked. "How you doing, LeNard?"

LeNard's moon face slowly widened into a smile, a gold tooth gleaming proudly at the forefront. "I'm alright, man," he said. "Long time, no see, my brother."

I decided to suck up. "Y'all know it wasn't my idea to go over there to school with the crackers," I said. "You know it was my daddy that sent me over there. But damn, I got to come back here with my people to hear Smokey Robinson and James Brown. Over there, I ain't seen a Black girl in so long, Mahlon's starting to look good to me."

They both laughed. Ralph was a real ladies' man, a subject about which LeNard was clueless.

Ralph turned around at the pulsating beat of James Brown singing "I Feel Good."

"Hey, sorry fellas,"Ralph said, "I gots to dance with me one of these fine sisters." Ralph walked confidently across the floor and asked another former classmate of mine, Regina Lawson, to dance. Regina, tall as Ralph, was known to be on the fast side. She and Ralph, the first couple on the dance floor, started swinging, cool and collected. The floor soon filled up.

LeNard and I watched. I asked him if his Dad was going to be selling barbeque at the fair (as he regularly did) in a couple of weeks and he said, "Yeah." We continued to watch in stupid silence. Mitty Collier's "I Had a Talk With My Man Last Night" came on. Ralph and Regina went into the mutual clutch of the soul slow dance.

I glanced at the girls sitting along the wall. Most of my socializing had been with the Jack And Jill crowd, but none of that crowd was there. I was afraid if I asked a girl I didn't know to dance, I'd get turned down. And to walk across the floor to where the girls sat and then get turned down made you feel like everyone's attention and scorn was heaped on you in that moment of shame. It could be beyond humbling.

So I stood there like a jerk and watched. Ralph, in one of his intermittent breaks came over and said to me, "Boy, ain't no girl gon' come over here and ask your lame ass to dance. You better get yo' White-boy dressing ass over there and ask one of them girls to dance."

"I am, man; I am," I said. I sure wanted a dance. But I just stood there next to LeNard hoping I didn't look as pathetic as I felt.

As the dance approached its end at 11:30, I had, after much furtive evaluation, picked one out. Her name was Philippa Moseby and she was a senior. I knew who she was because my friend, Spencer, had talked about her and many other girls as we rode around our neighborhood on our bikes and later in his ugly little Chevy.

Spencer's and mine was an interesting friendship given that he was two years my senior and had graduated the year before. It had started during the several years that Spencer, a decorated Explorer scout, had worked with my Boy Scout troop, over which my dad had served as troop leader.

"She's quiet," he'd told me, "Ain't ever got that much to say." "But why you asking about Phillipa? You know she's way too dark for you rich-ass Black folk," he said jokingly-I thought.

Spencer, whose opinion of himself was higher than anyone else's, had once confided that he would have "tapped" Phillipa, but she was "too thin" for him.

I remember saying, "Yeah, right," all the while doubting that he'd ever "tapped" anybody. "She's not too dark for me, I think she's fine."

She was dark, though. Her skin was the color of chocolate pudding. And from what I had seen of her, her disposition was as smooth as her skin. She had a coolness about her. I'd noticed that she had not been out on the dance floor much; and I'd seen her turn down Troy Johnson, the cocky quarterback for the Baby Rattlers, when he'd asked her to dance on a slow song. I knew I'd not seen Philippa dance on a slow song but I had made a pact with myself that I was going to ask her to slow dance before the lights came on.

As I tried to pump up my courage, the lights started to flash, the blink was shocking, triggering a near-panic in my semi-desperate mind. I started walking toward her, hoping to be close enough to her to extend my hand to her first, because all the boys, even the confirmed wallflowers, wanted that last chance to get next to a real live girl before going home to their dreams.

The sweet high notes of the Impressions' "I'm So Proud" began to ooze from the speakers. I found myself directly in front of her. She was talking to her friend, probably, like most girls, trying to seem disinterested before the expected rush of the young bucks.

I reached out my hand and asked too quickly and too loudly, "Would you like to dance?" She looked up at me; so did her chubby friend. I mean, I had materialized, basically out of thin air and, in my desperation, had almost yelled the question. She looked at her friend, and back at me. In those micro seconds, I knew that my dignity was on front-street for her to destroy. It was, in my mind, like the scene was being shot under water. She took my hand and got up. Damn, I was happy as a man with a new job. That very moment could only be appreciated by one who'd laid a big part of himself on the line, and won. At sixteen, asking Phillipa Moseby to slow dance on "I'm So

Proud," was to me the equivalent of slaying a small dragon.

I led her, still holding her hand, toward the middle of the floor. I pressed my right hand lightly, but firmly, on her back. For a lame Jack and Jiller, I could slow dance pretty well. On a rare occasion when my eyes actually focused, I saw Phillippa's petulant, overweight girlfriend looking intently at us and nodding her head in our direction as she whispered animatedly to another heavy girl one seat down.

I went back into blissful oblivion. Let them whisper, let them all whisper. At that point in time, the building could have burned down, but as long as the Impressions' sang "I'm So Proud" I would have continued to dance with Phillippa Moseby.

To my utter dismay, the Impressions ceased singing about how proud they were. Oh so reluctantly, I released my vice-like grip around her waist. She stepped back and looked me directly in my eyes. Although my dance with Phillipa had me wanting to ask her if she wanted to get engaged, I realized in a moment of clarity that I hadn't said a thing to her after shouting out my request for a dance. "Thank you." I said in all my lameness.

She smiled, her teeth white and even. "You're welcome," she said. "You don't need to walk me back to my seat. My name is Phillipa."

"I know," I said, "My name is Keith." I wanted to say more but she turned lightly and walked back to her chubby friend who, with a sour expression, was holding Phillipa's coat and looking at her watch.

No matter how I tried, I couldn't shake the memory of Phillipa. I wanted to call her, but I did not know if that would ever happen. Over and above not knowing her phone number, I didn't know whether she would be receptive to a call from me. But I guess no degree of fear could get between me and my hormones. I was on a mission that could only be accomplished when I got a chance to talk to Phillipa.

I knew where I could get help. I called Spencer. He'd graduated in the same class with Phillippa's brother. After getting him on the phone, I didn't waste any time.

"Spence, I want to call Phillippa Moseby," I said. "Do you know her number?"

"Boy, you something," he started off condescendingly. "Girl

slow dance with your lame ass one time and you're already stalking her."

I had to put up with his crap. "Come on man," I implored. "What's her mother's last name and what street do they live on?"

"Alright my boy," he chuckled, clearly enjoying himself. "Her mom's name is Jenifer White and they live on Douglas Avenue. You can look it up from there." He continued, "I don't even know why you even bothering with that girl, man. You know Eagle (short for "bald eagle" as my friends referred to my dad) and Della don't want you messing with no Black girl from the Flats—you know that!"

Annoyed, I said through clinched teeth, "I'm not worried about that, Spence. Thanks for your help."

A couple of minutes later, I was looking at her number, trying to grow some courage. I thought to myself, if I could go play football in Monticello, I should have the courage to dial up Phillippa Moseby. I tried to get the negative thoughts out of mind: like her asking me who I was or why I was calling her. What did I really want? That was an appropriate question. I thought for a second. I wanted to see her again.

I dialed. A woman answered the phone. "May I speak to Phillippa, please?" I said in my most polite voice. Long pause.

"Who's calling?" Her voice was borderline rude.

"This is Keith Neyland."

"Keith who?" she practically snarled.

"Neyland," I repeated.

She said nothing. After a pause, a distinctly sweeter voice got on the phone. "Hello, this is Phillippa."

I took a deep breath. "Phillippa, this is Keith Neyland. We met at the dance last Friday," I started to ramble. "You remember I danced with you on the last record?"

"Yes, Keith, I remember you," she sounded sweet, if non-committal. My mind went into overdrive, I did not want there to be even the briefest period of silence.

I rambled on. "I go to Florida High but went to Lucy Moten and A&M Junior High (both schools in the FAMU demonstration school system) from fourth grade through eighth; I'm a junior now ...I know you're a senior." I paused to catch my breath.

She jumped in, "You know, now that I think back, I kind of remember you as being in the grade behind me. So, why'd you to go to that White school in the first place?" she inquired.

I'd been asked this a few times before and had a stock answer. "My Dad sent me over there so I could learn to compete with White people since, he said, I'll probably be competing with them the rest of my life."

"I don't think I could handle it over there," she said. "I couldn't take always getting called out my name."

I was getting more confident, "It is hard to get used to, but I've gotten to the point that I can tune a lot of that name-calling stuff out. It's a lot worse playing basketball or football on away games." I was pumped that I could so quickly let her know I was a jock.

"Oh, you play sports," she said.

"I play football, basketball, and run track–I was the State Champ in the 440 yard run last year."

Though subtle, her voice sounded as though she was impressed. She seemed to be enjoying our conversation, especially when it centered on sports. Kind of abruptly, however, she said, "I've got to get off the phone now, my mother wants to use it."

About a minute before she had ended her conversation with Keith, Phillippa's mother had come and stood right in front of her and mouthed that she needed to use the phone. This struck Phillipa as odd since her mother very rarely called anyone.

When Philippa hung the phone up, her mother looked directly into her eyes and asked, "So what did 'Mr. Richboy' want?"

"Mom, all he wanted to do was talk to me."

"Well I don't like it," her mother said. "Boys like him don't mean girls like you no good."

"Why do you say that, Ma?" Phillippa asked. "You think boys here in the Flats mean me or any of my girlfriends any good?"

As she turned around to walk away, Phillippa's mother looked over her shoulder, "I know those Lee Manor boys don't want nothing but what they can get off girls from the Flats. Leave that boy alone." She turned and continued walking away.

"Hey Ma," Phillippa said, as her mother walked away. "I thought you had to use the phone?"

Without looking back, her mother said, "I'll call 'em back later."

I called her again two days later. Again, her mother answered the phone with an attitude that clearly indicated that she did not think any more highly of me than she had when I'd called the first time. But Phillippa seemed pleased to hear from me. We talked about a number of topics starting with our favorite school subjects, what we did in our spare time, and movies. She casually allowed that she did not see a lot of movies except on those occasions when her "boyfriend" took her to the movies on A&M's campus.

"Boyfriend, you have a boyfriend?" I stammered, the ease by which she'd dropped the bomb on me having momentarily confused me.

"Yeah, Keith, I've been dating Andre, a sophomore at A&M from Tampa, for the past three months."

Her declaration of her relationship status was even more stinging because it was made with obvious pride. I felt like the wind had been knocked out of me. I felt hurt, stupid, and angry in equal doses. I wanted to ask her why she hadn't mentioned her college boyfriend earlier but chose not to. She might have told me it wasn't my business and she would have been right, I guess.

I had nothing else to say. "I will talk to you later, Philippa," I said abruptly.

She had to have known that her having a boyfriend had been devastating to me, but she breezily answered, "Okay, Keith, Good night."

I hung the phone up and searched for perspective. First, I was dumped by Bennetta, and now my latest love interest had cavalierly advised me that, in view of her college boyfriend, she was uninterested in a lame high school junior. I realized that I had two strikes and couldn't help wondering if strike three was in my future. I knew that I was in no hurry to find out.

A week following the dance, I found myself standing alone on the goal line of the Monticello High football field awaiting the opening kickoff in my first varsity game. My state of mind had not been helped when I had first run out on the field because at that time the Monticello band had decided to break into a spirited rendition of Dixie accompanied by loud rebel yells.

I waited as the opening kickoff- long and strong- tumbled out of the sky into my waiting hands. After watching the ball into my hands, I looked up and two Monticello Tigers were right there ready to pounce. I could actually see the glee in their eyes. They hit me simultaneously from opposite sides which had the effect of "standing me up" for what seemed like forever. All of a sudden I felt the ball being jerked from my hands. I realized that I had fumbled and that one of the Monticello players was running into the end zone for a touchdown. As the Monticello crowd cheered loudly, I got up off the ground. I was devastated. I had not only let my teammates down-frankly, I could live with that-but I had let Black folks down by underscoring in the minds of racists that we cave in under pressure. I started jogging over to our sideline; no one looked at me, nor said anything. I knew the vocal racists on my own team were going to have a field day with the fact that the Nigger had choked under pressure and fumbled the opening kickoff.

I stood alone on the sideline in my shame. All of a sudden Coach Rose walked over to me and told me to get back on the field. I realized I was running back out to, once again, be the center return man on our kick receiving formation. For an instance, I thought that maybe I hadn't just fumbled; but as I got to the middle of the field, I heard a high-pitched scream, "Make that Coon cough it up again." I had to realize then that I had, in fact, fumbled the opening kick-off and the Demons were as a result down 7-0. The second kickoff was not nearly as high. I caught it and ran several steps to my left before I was tackled. As I hit the ground, I couldn't believe it, the ball squirted away again. I lunged for it, but to my horror, I saw it gobbled up by a pair of White arms. A split second later, I realized that the White arms extended from a maroon and white Florida High uniform. I was ecstatic that we had recovered my second fumble as I ran to our sideline until I was confronted by a visibly angry Coach Rose who snarled at me, " Keith, hold on to the goddamn ball."

From my vantage point standing alone on the sideline, I watched the two North Florida Class B powerhouses slug it out. At halftime, I had not gotten back into the game and the score remained 7-0. Coming out to the field after halftime, Coach Rose walked over to me and, looking directly into my eyes, growled: "You got to hang on to that damn ball." "I know Coach", I lamely replied. He went on. " Look, Keith we're gonna try that tight-end sweep pass to you in our first series. Go get me a touchdown; You owe me one, Lightening.

True to his word, on a 3rd and 4 on their 47 yard line, Coach Rose called for me to get in there for our starting split-end, Robin Hatheway. As I ran onto the field, as I expected, the murmur from the Monticello crowd got louder with the usual epithets. I heard two

Monticello coaches yell to their defensive backs: "Watch 24." I couldn't help noting that "24" was the best name I'd been called all night by anyone from Monticello. I was making progress I thought to myself.

As our QB barked out the snap count, I saw that two defensive backs who were apparently assigned to cover me were giving me a ten yard cushion; I couldn't help wondering why they assumed that I warranted that much respect. I thought to myself that while they might not know it yet, they were about to find out that their respect for me was warranted. When the ball was snapped, I took off low and hard at the defensive backs. Eight yards downfield I briefly slowed and feinted and swiveled my head to the right, but then planted my foot and took off at full speed for the goalposts. As I was running my pattern, our 6' 5" tight end, Karl Weiss, was coming around on a tight-end sweep. He stopped, and threw a perfect spiral into the night as I streaked down the middle of the field. I saw the ball coming down to me while I was in perfect stride. I never, even for a moment, entertained the thought of dropping it (I later told the father of one of my teammates that if I had dropped it, I would have continued running until I got to Tallahassee.) I watched it into my hands and crossed the goal line. Before I knew it, Karl was in the end zone giving me a big hug. I could see players and coaches jumping around patting each other on the backs on our sidelines.

A few players that had up to that point ignored me came up and awkwardly told me I'd made a nice catch. For that sweet moment, I noticed that the theretofore boisterous Monticello crowd was quiet as church mice. I felt a sense of redemption. Nevertheless we lost 21-20 when our normally steady kicker blew a PAT. After the game, Coach Rose allowed me to ride back to Tallahassee in my uniform with my dad. It was a great reprieve given that I would have been sitting on the bus on a seat all by myself for the 26-mile ride back to Tallahassee as I had on the ride up to Monticello. (Tim who set with me sometimes often set with his friend our fullback, John Killien). It was truly a relief to be riding along with my dad away from Monticello. I got the sense that my dad was feeling the same way.

I didn't play a lot the last three games of the season, although I did take a punt 40 yards for a touchdown against Madison High. At his unimaginative best, Coach Rose would normally send me in on third and longs, split me out and send me deep. I couldn't get behind any of the defensive backs who were all giving me fifteen yard cushions as if I were Bob Hayes.

Football season ended the next Friday with a home game against crosstown rival Ricketts High. I was in the game for six plays. Only two were worth remembering. The first involved me setting up to return a punt. The ball was kicked straight up, and I waited to catch it with no fair catch sign. Two of their guys clobbered me (that was starting to get old) as soon as I caught it, but I didn't fumble. Their crowd cheered as if they had scored a touchdown.

My next moment occurred when, on third-and-long, surprise, surprise, I went deep. Our quarter back pumped like he was throwing to me deep and slipped the ball into the waiting arms of our running back, Doug Mullins who burst through the center of the line and veered toward the sideline where he was about to get tackled by their best player, a big, fast, mean linebacker who had Doug in his sights and was crouching as he closed in, ready to lower the boom.

Alas, that's where I came into play having circled back to the action. Given that in his preparing to hit Doug, he was thoroughly oblivious to my approach, I de-cleated him hitting him high with my best shot. He fell backward and Doug scored. I got more congrats from my teammates for that block than I had for my touchdown catch in Monticello. And with that, my junior year's mostly forgettable football season ended.

The following Monday, I was in the gym with almost twenty other aspiring basketball players. I was happy to see Mahlon at 6'1"and Mike who had grown to my height, 5'11", after attending a two week basketball camp at Duke were he had developed into a very good player. Lonnie, having his game face on, barely acknowledged me.

There were three footballers going out for the team-Karl Weiss, the centerpiece of the team, Robin Hathaway, a 6'1" guard-forward destined for substantial pine time, and me. I didn't know where I stood in Coach Albertson's plans for building his team. I, like virtually everyone else, knew that there were essentially two positions open-point guard, and small forward. Karl at 6'5" and Frank Wattenberger at 6'3" were locks, as was a new transfer from Raleigh, North Carolina, Bill Clayton, a 6' sweet shooter who had played extensively for his school in Raleigh and whose game-I'd been told by Mike and Mahlon-was tight and highly favored by Coach

Albertson.

After running some drills, Coach Albertson picked ten of us to play five-on-five shirts and skins. Karl was designated as a Skin, along with Wattenberger and Clayton. As he prepared to call out the names of the other two Skins, he had everyone's rapt attention because the next two names would be tentative starters. "Okay, Robin and Keith," he said.

That was that, I was starting. Karl and I played the entire scrimmage as a "skins" and Coach substituted Mike, Mahlon, and Lonnie. I had to admit to myself that starting had been a huge goal of mine-one that I'd been concerned about given my pine time on Varsity as a sophomore versus the considerable playing experience that Mahlon, Mike and Lonnie had garnered on JV. I smiled to myself. I guessed that all my Varsity pine time and my daily practice against our Varsity players had been worth it. Funny how that worked out.

Our first game was against Havana High, the only school in the small town of Havana, Florida, which was about twenty-five miles northwest of Tallahassee. Though I didn't know it at the time, Havana High was known for having a solid basketball program-probably because it was the only sport they played. Though they had no one as tall as the 6'5" Weiss, they had three starters who were around 6'2" and they were pretty well-built and looked quite athletic-like serious hoopsters.

Before the game started, I got a bit of a thrill when our starting five was introduced. Though this had been a time-honored tradition at Florida High hoop games, I'd barely noticed it last year, given my pine-brother status and the fact that I already knew our starters. But hearing my name called and running out to the foul line while our fans cheered was rich.

When the game started, the Havana Bears proved to be very worthy opponents. They played hard, and they did not back down an inch-they got right up in our faces and tried to play a suffocating man-to-man defense. Little did they know, however, that playing me so close played right into my limited skill set. It allowed me to do the one thing I did well-drive, especially right. And I did a lot of that that night. I'd receive a pass and then establish a pivot foot from which I'd rock-either faking like I was going up for a shot, or driving left, or both-before I took off with a quick first step right and drove to the basket before finishing with a baby hook off glass into the hoop. I made three baskets using that technique, hit a jumper and was 4 of 5 from the foul line. My 15 points made me the highest scorer on our team that night in a tight game we won by five-54 to 49.

My next game the following Friday wasn't nearly as good. For that game, we went to Jasper, Florida to play a team we were clearly better than. While I scored 10 points, I missed three breakaway layups off steals because I couldn't for the life of me make a layup running full speed right at our basket. After the Havana game, I thought all my layups had to be baby hooks off the glass rather than picking a spot on the backboard and simply laying it in.

After my first four games, I was all over the place with my scoring-15, 10, 5, 2. The two-point game, which had been against cross-town rival Ricketts, was particularly galling. There were several Black students in attendance including, much to my dismay, Bennetta. I guess they'd come because, along with me playing in the Varsity game, two Black students from Ricketts-both Jack & Jillers-were playing on the Junior Varsity team, which went up against FHS's JV before the Varsity game.

Whatever the reason, I couldn't get it out of my mind that Bennetta would be there watching me play. I don't know why her presence at the game meant so much given her callous treatment in publicly dumping me. Until that night, I had convinced myself that I was totally over her, especially with the attention I had been giving Phillippa. But Bennetta's presence, in all her undeniable cuteness, made me feel that she was the only one in the stands, and that she was just watching me. I tried to play extra-special great, but because of my self-imposed pressure, I found myself choking throughout the game.

Ricketts beat us by four points. We could have won fairly easily if I'd shot better than 1 for 5, but I didn't. I played as if I was scared to mess-up-passively and tight. I hurried off the court when the game ended, rushed to shower, dressed, and hurried out to the parking lot where my dad was waiting.

"Tough night," he commented.

As we drove out of the lot, I said, "I know, I just couldn't relax and play my game tonight."

My dad was cool; he never really criticized my sports abilities. But on this night, he said, "You had no aggressiveness tonight."

"Yeah, I just couldn't seem to get in the flow."

He smiled. "I bet seeing Bennetta in the stands didn't help."

I had to smile back, he knew exactly what had been my problem. "I guess it was pretty obvious, huh?"

He took one of his hands off the steering wheel, made a fist and playfully hit me on my shoulder. "Shake it off, my man," he said. "You'll do better next game."

My dad was the best.

When I got home, my mother made me a tuna fish sandwich, which I wolfed down with two big glasses of red Kool-Aid. In my mind, nothing quenched a thirst like Kool-Aid, especially red Kool-Aid.

My mom sat at the table and talked with my dad and, as she was sometimes wont to do, watched me eat. Although she'd undoubtedly listened to the game on the radio, I volunteered to her, "We lost."

"Don't worry," she said. "You'll win the next one."

Three weeks into the season I was in a mini-slump on the hoop court-my outside shot had never been consistent, and had gotten worse. So I had major self-doubt about whether I could score enough to be an asset to the team. I had no such doubt about my ability to play defense and I planned to unleash my defensive fury on our next opponent Greenville and their star Orville Noble. Noble with his slump shouldered build and slew-footed gait was nevertheless a deadly shooter averaging 24 points a game.

"I bet he won't get 10 points tonight," I said to the Rhaney boys. It was way out of character for me to brag like that, but somewhere deep inside I was trying to shore up my confidence.

I can definitively report that Noble did not get 10 points as I predicted he wouldn't. No, while making better use of screens during the second half, he scored a total of 31 and that was after I had blocked his first two jumpers and had held him to 7 points in the first half.

After the game, Mahlon and Mike didn't comment on the fact that Noble, a slump-shouldered slew footed player, had lit me up like a Christmas tree in the second half. I didn't get much solace from their silence and wound up seeing Noble swish 17-footers in my sleep that night.

The first week of February found us scheduled to play Leon High School at Tully Gym on Florida State's campus. Talk about David versus Goliath-Leon had a student population of 1800 students while FHS had less than 400. It was the single game on our schedule that meant the most to us. I felt-and believed my teammates did also-that while we had a chance to win (albeit a small one), we could, more likely, continue the tradition of getting blown out by Leon.

The extent of my optimism was based upon the fact that, despite Leon's infinitely larger pool of male students to draw from, we were going to be the taller team-largely because of our 6'5" center Karl Weiss. Leon had lost its two tall centers from the previous year to graduation. Against us, their two tallest starters were 6'3". On the other hand, my pessimism was based on the new addition to Leon's team, one Tommy Curtis, a Black, 6-foot dynamo who was averaging more than 25 points through Leon's first seven games against Class AA competition. Not only was he a scoring machine, but he also did all of his scoring with great flamboyance-he constantly talked as he played, telling defenders how futile their efforts were going to be ("You can't guard me, the Secret Service can't guard me."). From what I'd heard, he always loved to put on a show-starting with the "Big Tommy Curtis" he had boldly stenciled on both of his sneakers.

Tallahassee's newspaper, "The Democrat", expressly noted that Tommy and I would be the first Negroes to play varsity basketball for our respective schools. The related article promised that the two of us would likely guard each other, given Tommy's scoring prowess and my reputed defensive skills. Next to the story was a close-up picture of me. I realized that mine could have been the first picture of a Black high school athlete ever printed on the front page in the Democrat's Sports Section. I couldn't help wondering if Bennetta and Philippa had seen it. In any event, I know I'd never felt as special as that picture made me feel.

Game night was electric. The crowd was noticeably larger than it had been the previous year and, surprisingly, there were sprinklings of Black spectators all around the gym. I noticed that, on the Florida High side of the gym, there was almost an entire section of bleachers seating Demon football players uniformed in their letter-man jackets. Included in their midst were Duke and his cadre of football-playing Kluxxers.

As I ran with my teammates on the court, I looked over at Duke and his boys wondering whether they would be rooting for our team to win despite how much he and his boys hated me. Noticing that Duke and his group enthusiastically followed the cheering commands of the cheerleading squad, it appeared that they had an overriding dedication to the athletic success of dear old FHS. Who knew?

As I and my team ran out on the court and began our lay-up drills, I couldn't help but glance over at the Leon team, especially at Tommy. He seemed to always be in motion, even standing in the lay-up line he was continually moving-clapping his hands, shaking his arms, bouncing up and down on his toes and running his mouth apparently to no one in particular. He exuded confidence. I couldn't help compare his virtual command that people look at him to my overall self-consciousness that tightened me up just thinking about people possibly looking at me.

As I ran in to make a practice lay-up, I told myself that if I allowed my self-consciousness to negatively impact my game, Tommy would happily embarrass the hell out of me. The thought of being embarrassed by Tommy in front of all those people was not acceptable. Realizing that Tommy couldn't know the paralyzing fear I felt awaiting the game's start, I decided to play as aggressively and as hard as I ever had before-I resolved that I would try my best to project confidence whether I actually had it or not.

Just before the game, I had a new experience before an athletic contest. I shook hands with an opposing player for the first time ever when Tommy stepped over to me and gave me a soul handshake. Smiling, he said, "Let's give these White folks a show."

I couldn't help but think how cool that was. But as he stepped away after our shake, he said, "But you better know, Keith, there's no way you can guard me. I'm gonna get mine." Still smiling, he bounced away with a walk that was all pigeon-toes and moving parts.

I did play hard that night and stayed in Tommy's face. I made every effort to deny him the ball. It was my challenge to minimize the time he had the ball and I could see within the first five minutes (during which he'd taken only three rushed, inaccurate shots) that he'd dropped his perpetual, arrogant smile and was starting to frown. On a rare occasion early in the game, they set up in a half-court 1-3-1 offense with Tommy at the point. I got into a good defensive posture in front of him-close, but not so close that I'd be vulnerable to his drives. I remembered Coach Albertson's directive to guard him as close as I could without fouling.

As he faked left, and attempted to drive by me, I crouched low. I flicked my right hand across his body, knocked the ball behind him, grabbed the ball, and took off full-speed for our hoop. It seemed as though I was halfway to our hoop when I realized the ref had blown his whistle, indicating I'd fouled. I couldn't believe it as I stopped and turned around. But I wasn't mad at the call because I knew-and Tommy knew-that the steal had been clean.

After the steal, Tommy seemed to press even more and rush his shots. When he did manage to shoot, my hand was always in his face. It wasn't aesthetically a well-played game, but we played together-and with scrappiness. Our big, raw-boned center, Karl, owned the boards and when he got an offensive rebound, they were helpless in stopping him from going back up to score or get fouled.

We won 58-53, and I had never been happier in winning any game anywhere. Karl scored 23 points, and I was our next highest scorer with 11. Tommy got seven. As I walked off the court, I saw Tommy sobbing uncontrollably in the arms of his mother. As I slowly panned the rest of the gym, I saw Duke and his boys jumping around and slapping each other on the back-thrilled that dear old FHS had won, even though I had been instrumental in that victory.

During the two weeks after the Leon game, we were scheduled to play two games against my buddies at Perry High School-the first in Perry and the second at our place. I could not have dreaded a trip to Perry any more, particularly given their general hatred toward Black people and their all-too specific hatred of me. I resolved not to think about the Perry game, but I knew its approach was inexorable.

I had kind of hoped Perry's officials would un-invite the integrated Demons, as I had been uninvited to play the JV game down there. But on a February Friday night, my teammates and I ran out on the floor of the old bandbox gym of Perry High. It was so small, it seemed like fans were on the court with us, which meant that crowd commentary was unfortunately highly audible to everyone on the court. As a result, I was the subject of a bevy of highly-audible epithets. The name-calling was vicious, and because of the close proximity of the fans, the intensity of their collective hatred was worse than even Monticello-and that was saying something. Indeed, the Perry student body seemed more hard–rural-and poorer-looking than anywhere we played.

Compounding my fears, once the game started, the player I was guarding insisted on taking every opportunity to look me in my eyes and aggressively call me Nigger. Up and down the court, even when he was dribbling the ball, he was constantly "Nigger-ing" me-even in front of the refs who did nothing. He was a muscular guy about an inch taller and twenty pounds heavier than me with a tough–looking demeanor, and throughout the game he seemed on the edge of violence.

We played a disjointed game that night, probably because our big man, Karl, had not made the trip to Perry because his 6' 5" body was beat up by flu symptoms. Thus, we clearly lacked our physical advantage in the middle of our offense. But considering the pervasive hostility in the little Perry gym, I couldn't help but feel, more importantly, that we were missing our combative champion.

The game itself was a ragged mess. I felt intimidated to a degree by the hostile environment including the constant badgering by the player I guarded. Our game plan missed Karl, and they were a loosely-coached bunch who, nevertheless, played us as if it was life or death. The player I guarded was a decent athlete, though not an accomplished hoopster. In any event, we were leading by 4 near the end of the third quarter when the player I guarded intercepted a lazy pass to me from Bill Clayton and took off dribbling frantically and moving at top-speed toward his basket. I was instantly placed in a dilemma: let the guy take it in, given the jump he'd had on any chance I had to catch him, or run like hell to make a defensive play at the basket

I chose the latter. I took out after him hard and ran him down just as he went up for his lay-up. I could see that he had relaxed at the basket and was going up to drop the ball over the front of the rim. I'm sure it seemed to him that I came out of nowhere and blocked his shot. My momentum carried me in front of the guy and he ran into me and pushed me into the padding on the wall just behind the basket.

"Fuck you, Nigger," he said through clenched teeth as he took a step backward and brought up his fists and started stepping toward me.

I immediately put my hands up and crouched in a comfortable boxing posture. I wasn't going to stand there with my hands down and let him pummel me. For a guy not known for toughness, I felt no fear. I thought I could take pretty good care of myself. I must have looked ready and able to do just because the guy stopped his approach.

"Calm down, Ronnie, it's not worth it," said the ref while rushing between us. I couldn't help notice the ref had called the guy by his first name.

After directing us to our coaches, the refs came over and announced that we were both ejected from the game. I complained to Coach Albertson that I hadn't thrown a punch but had merely gotten into a boxing stance so that the guy who had been antagonizing me all game could not just come up and slug me in the face. I noticed that Coach had not responded, and that he looked shockingly preoccupied. I then realized why-the crowd.

The Perry fans were at a fever pitch, yelling loudly and collectively: "Get that Nigger!"

The ejected Perry player and I were sent back to the locker room. A Sheriff's Deputy who materialized out of nowhere walked with me back to the locker room. The crowd continued to unload on me unmercifully. Chancing a quick glance at the jeering Perry students, I noticed that one of the most egregious offenders was literally as dark as Mahlon. The student saw me make eye contact with him and immediately shot me the finger to go along with his name-calling. The student wasn't even totally White but was among the loudest of the vocal bigots. I couldn't help wondering how that worked.

We lost a close game that night, but my most vivid memory was the small crowd of Perry fans who stayed and loudly jeered us as we walked to our bus. In my mind, they were a mob, and I knew that history was replete with unpleasantness between White mobs and Black folks. I was happy to see the two police cars parked next to our bus. It was the quietest bus ride I'd ever taken.

Overall, my junior basketball season was a success. We finished 16-9, and we were conference champs. But there were two games later in the season that made our season that much more special. We beat Leon at their brand new gym for our first sweep of them-perhaps ever; and we avenged our loss against Perry in our last home game of the season.

The second Leon game was actually a sweeter victory than the first. Tommy had proclaimed to mutual friends that our first win against them had been a fluke and that our team in general-and I specifically-were overrated. He'd promised everyone who'd listen that they would crush the Class B Demons, and he would score at least 30 points.

As it turned out, we played a better game against them the second time around. We were better at spreading the scoring around. I scored 16, and Karl had 19. Tommy played much better, but only scored 16.

At the end of the game, he came over to me dry-eyed and extended his hand. "Great game, Keith," he said. "But you'd better be better next year 'cause I promise you I will be." (As it turned out, he was better his junior and senior seasons. By his senior year, he was named the Number 1 basketball player in the state of Florida, and he received a scholarship to play basketball at UCLA where he played with a fellow named Walton.)

Our home Perry game was fun, starting with our traditional walk through the gym to our locker room at halftime of the JV game. As usual at home games, our team was dressed in our burgundy blazers with ties. Mahlon, Mike, and I were last in the procession of players walking directly in front of the visiting Perry fans to the gym door leading to our locker room. I thought the three of us looked nice in our blazers, creased slacks, and well-shined loafers.

As we passed within a couple of arms' length of their crowd, I expected to hear some of what I'd heard the week before in Perry. But I heard nothing; there was total silence as I felt their eyes following us.

As the game started, I saw that the guy who had been ejected with me from the Perry game had not made the trip to Tallahassee. While I didn't know why he was absent, my dad had informed me that he had received a call from an official from the Conference Committee the Monday following the earlier Perry game. The Conference Committee monitored, among other things, the compliance of member teams with its rules and regulations. In any event, the official had told Dad that the Committee had tentatively decided to suspend me for the rest of the season for "fighting" in the

Perry game. Dad told me that he had advised the man that there had been no fighting by me; I was merely a player who was charged by an opponent aggressively and had merely defended himself from a potential assault.

Dad further told me that he had advised the official that he would "sue the pants off" the Committee if it tried to suspend his boy for one minute-especially when the refs who ultimately answered to the Committee had allowed the aggressor on the Perry team to racially harass his son throughout the game. There was never any further talk about suspending me. I couldn't help but tease Dad a bit: "Sue the pants off the Committee…"

We beat Perry easily the second time around, behind my twenty points. During Spring football practice several months later, as I casually stood on the sideline playing catch with our second-team QB, I saw a figure approaching me dressed in the maroon shorts and T-shirt worn by the FSU freshman football team, which was practicing at the other end of the field. Imagine my surprise when I saw that the approaching player was none other than the Perry player who had antagonized me, and with whom I'd been ejected from the game. Not knowing his intentions, I quickly threw the ball back to our QB and turned to face the young man from Perry. He strode up to me-right in front of me. I remembered to try to be ready for a punch from the right or left hand. But he didn't throw a punch; he reached out his hand for me to shake and said, "Keith, I'm sorry about the stuff that happened down in Perry. I'm the son of a Baptist minister, and I knew then and for sure know now that nobody deserves to be treated like I treated you down there. I ask that you forgive me."

Shaking his hand, I said, "Look, man, I appreciate your apology and for what it's worth, I forgive you."

He smiled, as if he'd just had an audience with the Pope, or the Baptist equivalent and jogged back to his teammates.

Track season started immediately after my junior basketball season. It should be noted that, despite how my story has read thus far, my whole high school life was not solely focused on sports, academics and failed romances.

Late in my sophomore year, while attending a school assembly, I sat daydreaming during an informal ceremony during which Key Club members announced the names of each newly selected member. I perked up when I heard Tim Garland's name called. While I knew little about the Key Club (it's a junior auxiliary of the Kiwanis Club) except that it appeared to be quite an honor to its members, I did remember how decent the club had been in trying to transition Mahlon and me into the newly-integrated FHS.

As Tim's name was read, the accompanying applause was enthusiastic-as it had been for the couple of names called previously.

"Keith Neyland," the Key Club member read off next. I became momentarily disoriented. I hadn't heard my name, had I? I concluded that I had to have been mistaken until my right shoulder was tapped by one of the members. Like the other inductees, I stood up and followed him to the stage where the other inductees were lined up.

To the extent I noticed, my applause was significantly less enthusiastic. I stood there in front of the Florida High student body trying not to focus individually on any of the students. I knew so many of the faces would manifest incredulity–the nerve of the Key Club in selecting one of "them" before any of the otherwise eligible White boys. But that was that. I was, as a sophomore, a member of the Key Club-certainly the only one of color in North Florida and perhaps in the whole state. I knew I had Bob Sanchez, my sophomore English teacher and faculty sponsor .

It was an honor to be selected to be in the Key Club, and I attended meetings regularly, but I never felt comfortable, and never said much of anything. To me, any direct effort to assimilate smacked of Uncle Tom-ism and, as dumb as that might sound now, I couldn't shake in my mind that I didn't want to appear to be kissing up to them for acceptance-I could not live with the thought of being thought of in that manner-by them or by me.

During the early part of my junior year, I got involved, with little prior thought, in another extracurricular activity. I'd always liked creative writing and enjoyed class assignments to write short stories.

One day in English class, Mr. Sanchez, my favorite teacher, was called away for the entire class, but left instructions for us to read a short story for the duration of class. Having already read the story, I sat there and began a writing project, the nature of which just came to me as I sat there and wrote. It turned out to be a funky little imaginary piece that came to me out of nowhere. It detailed my hiding a tape recorder in the faculty lounge and describing the amusing (?) things I heard from various unnamed, though identifiable, faculty members and staff engaged in a number of peculiar activities, including the following: our bald assistant principal, Mr. Cole, counting brushstrokes as he brushed the surviving strands on the sides of his head, two of our most macho coaches watching and intently discussing a cloying soap opera, and a scenario where one of our Black janitors [called by his first name by all students-toward whom he was, in my view, always disgustingly obsequious] entered the lounge and started singing "Dixie."

When I finished, I'd completed a fairly long story of fictitious scenarios. I showed the piece to Mr. Sanchez and later that night to my dad, and he asked what I intended to do with it. I told him that I had thought about giving it to the school newspaper, The Trident, which I had begun to regularly read upon its publication every two weeks.

My dad thought that was a great idea, and he suggested that maybe I could write a regular column for which I'd need a title. Looking me directly in my eyes, he asked, "Could you write a column like this every couple of weeks, or more importantly, do you want to?" Mr. Sanchez who was The Trident's faculty sponsor was also encouraging.

It only took me a moment to respond, "Yeah, I think I can write a couple of columns a month and I would enjoy it."

I loved creative writing (almost as much as I hated public speaking), and I thought I had a good sense of humor. I wanted my fellow FHS students to know I was more than just a good athlete.

That night, I couldn't sleep. I mentally tossed around possible titles for my columns. By morning, I thought of the perfect one- "KKK: Keith's Kandid Komments." The following are two samples of my published columns.

Keith's Kandid Komments

by Keith Neyland

"REBEL" WITHOUT A CAUSE

At a time when it is popular for students to support various causes, I tried to think up one that I could advocate in my column. Since the possibilities seemed limited, I started looking through old issues of the TRIDENT for ideas and came across a column by an ex-Demon, Barry Handberg.

This column was on his bold attempt to find out whether Jefferson County was the last center of conservatism in Florida. Barry made a personal visit to that fine county for his information. He visited a couple of restaurants and a high school basketball game. He concluded that if traditions were changing, the rate was very, very slow.

I thought of attempting a follow-up on Barry's lead. However, his direct method of visiting the scene did not appeal to me. Not that it wouldn't be interesitng, even exciting, but it's just that track season is not quite here and I'm not a distance runner.

I then contemplated writing on the Free Speech Society at Florida High. While ours may not rival the University of California at Berkeley, you can believe that we have one and the headquarters are in the boys locker room. Of course, I shied away from writing an expose since many members are very big and given to emotional outburst.

I thought next of writing about all of the Young Liberals at Florida High. I really had plans to interview all of the members, but Dirk and Steve were busy.

I then considered taking up the cause of Adam Clayton Powell and his rift with Congress, but with both Democrats and Republicans against him, there aren't many left to "Keep the faith, baby!"

Since I was below par in some of my classes, I finally decided that the best cause for me to crusade for was higher pay for teachers---and for obvious reasons, hope for the best.

Keith's Kandid Komments

by Keith Neyland

The teachers of Florida are staging a mass walk-out because they are discontent with the plight of the teachers here in the State. They feel that this mass walk-out is the best way to dramatize their feelings and force a favorable solution to intolerable working conditions.

I have been giving considerable thought to the mass walk-out idea, and I have decided that it is a good technique which can be used by slum-dwellers in our large cities. Instead of rioting this summer to show discontent with intolerable conditions, these slum-dwellers should take a hint from the Florida teachers and peacably walk out of the slumbs and, let us say, camp in the suburbs.

Not that rioting doesn't have its assets. It immediately dramatizes and focuses attention on deplorable living conditions. Furthermore, you may possible get on TV and, of course, there are those new suits that you may have "picked-up". However, it also has its drawbacks. You nearly cut your hand off breaking that plate-glass window to get those new suits, and sure the TV cameras caught you, but as you were being led off to jail by that policeman who happened to be standing there when youwere going back for that new pair of shoes.

To put it simply, rioting is not the answer. I feel that if all the slum-dwellers would walk-out of the slums and refuse to return until conditions were greatly improve: they wold achieve more than if they just burned the slums down.

First of all, the slum landlords would raise a fuss with the city government because with all their tenants gone, there would be nobody to cheat. Next, the neighborhood businessmen would take their plea to city hall because with the slum population gone, there wold be nobody to exploit. Lastly, the population in suburbia would cry out to the city government for help because they are being infringed upon by the people they left the city to get away from in the frst place.

The walk-out in the big cities would even be easier than the one here in Florida. First of all, the slum-dwellers aren't under contract, and try as it may, the city can't replace the slums with substitutes.

The walk-out in the large northern cities may have problems that the teachers in Florida did not have. For one thing, it is likely that the governor will be at home.

So all of you, who through no fault of your own, are slum-dwellers, listen to me. Instead of rioting this summer, try the peaceful walk-out method. If it doesn't work—well, the next summer you may get that new pair of shoes after all.

Though I was not consulted in the utilization of the stick-figure logo associated with my column (depicting a Black stick-figure in a White Klan hood), I grew to like its irreverence in mocking that cowardly organization. My column was well received by the FHS student body and The Trident frequently referenced my column ("Read KKK in The Trident this week") in marketing its by-weekly publication.

Perhaps my most satisfying non-sports, extra-curricular activity occurred in early November my junior year. It was then that I learned by letter that I was to be inducted into the National Honor Society. The letter requested that I wear a suit and tie for the related assembly. I was ecstatic. This would be the opportunity for Mahlon and me (we had almost exactly the same GPA) to be identified before the whole school as smart-not just dumb Black boys who could jump high and run fast, like so many of them had been taught to believe. The NHS at Florida High was known to include the top students in a school renowned for having high academic standards.

So, as Mahlon and I were called on stage to be recognized, we knew that we would never completely rid all of our school mates of the stereotype of the dumb Black man. We knew, however, that our presence on that stage would, at minimum, cause the dyed-in-the-wool racists to rethink their ignorant generalizations; to us, that was incremental progress in our day-to-day experience of being prejudged.

Capping off the wonderful experience of being inducted, I looked out and saw standing in the back of the auditorium two brown faces-those of my parents beaming. I couldn't help noticing how well they were dressed: my mom in a beautiful, fashionable dress, and my dad in one of his sharply pressed suits with matching tie. I had certainly not expected to see them, and when the program ended, they rushed down the aisle to me as I did toward them and the three of us embraced with much back-slapping. I knew this honor meant more to them than even my most accomplished sports feat.

As the three of us were hugging, I noticed that we were in the midst of a mass of White students exiting the auditorium. I could see them walking by looking at us. In a split second, I realized that for the very first time at FHS, I was not self-conscious, I didn't care if they looked at me, I just hugged my parents that much harder.

Immediately after basketball season ended, I started practicing for track. With my status as the 440 State Champ, I found that I was not as enthused as the prior year. I had developed something of a different attitude-a new one for me: arrogance.

So, when our new track coach, interestingly known as Coach Whitey, informed us that he'd entered us into a city meet just two weeks after basketball ended, I beamed with confidence. Bring 'em on, I thought.

On the day of the meet, I walked around in my track togs and noticed a few of the athletes subtly pointing at me and whispering to each other. It made me walk taller. In the open quarter, I would show them how a state champion competed.

Lining up at the starting line, I glanced at the competition. Coach Whitey knew I was faster than the runners from Rickett's High and Godby High. He knew nothing about the one runner from Leon, but looking at his thin-almost frail-body and spindly legs, led me to believe that he did not present a threat. So, I felt invincible when the gun sounded and I took off.

As expected, despite the stagger, I found myself well ahead of the pack. I started to almost prance. This was fun; I was running away from everybody. At about the 330 mark, I felt the dreaded feeling of my upper body starting to tighten up-as if a baby bear had crawled on my back. As we headed down the back stretch, the bear had grown exponentially. My upper and lower body had tightened up as I futilely tried to maintain my speed.

I was no longer prancing; I was struggling to finish with some dignity, but I knew everyone could see the pain on my face and the decreasing coordination of my stride. Thirty or so yards from the finish line, I saw the Leon runner, frail legs and all, passing me on my side. I just watched because I had no chance of going any faster. When I followed him across the finish line, all I wanted to do was try like hell to catch my breath.

The victor walked over to me. "You're real good," he said. "I barely beat you, and I know you're just starting training for track after basketball."

I smiled and struggled through my heavy breathing to say, "Thanks."

Though I had an excuse for not running my best race, I was still humiliated. I realized that trying to face a challenge while steeped in arrogance, made a loss that much more devastating. I vowed that I would never assume that I was better than any other competitor-aiming to be self-confident, but not arrogant. The fall to reality was too steep and often too public.

About a month later, I wasn't surprised when Coach Whitey informed me that I would be running in the prestigious Florida Relays in Gainesville in a week and a half. He added to my surprise when he said, "It will be the hundred, not the quarter."

I got the sense that Coach just believed that folks of my hue were always well-suited for the hundred.

"You're eligible to participate because of the 10-flat you ran in the meet against Madison last week," he said. "So, you'll be eligible to run with the mostly small-school sprinters in the state with the winner moving up to run with the studs from south Florida."

Obviously having no choice in the matter, I mumbled, "Okay, coach."

I couldn't help remembering Barry's 9.5's and 9.6's. A last-place finish was a distinct possibility based on my pedestrian 10-flat.

On the day of the Florida Relays, just before the running of the small-school hundred, I stood in my lane and bent over, trying in vain to touch my toes, an exercise at which I'd never before been successful.

Glancing at my competitors, I saw one other was Black. I instantly thought that this race was winnable. I was confident that a bunch of White guys were not faster than me. Remembering my incredibly fast teammate, Barry Handburg, I rationalized that Barry had to have been an aberration or a light-skinned brother who passed. I obviously had forgotten the lesson in humility I'd received in getting beat running my first quarter earlier that year.

But as it turned out, I won the race-with a 9.9. I was ecstatic, and in about 20 minutes, I'd get to compete with the big dogs in the premier high school hundred-yard dash. I figured that with better competition, who knew how fast I could run?

At the starting blocks, looking at my competitors (who I'd heard were all from the Miami area), I noticed one thing: these guys (all but one being Black) looked fast. A couple of them were on the short side with big butts and massive thighs; the others were lean and sinewy with prototypical wide receiver builds-college wide receivers. I was in Lane 1 next to a short guy who looked like he could have had

200 pounds on a 5' 7" frame. He didn't look my way, but I noticed he had a toothpick in his mouth.

All my hints of arrogance had vanished only to be replaced by the apprehension of pending humiliation. Forcing myself to self-affirm, I told myself to get out of the blocks faster than them and run as fast as I could (not the most creative coaching advice).

Poised in our blocks, when the starter's gun sounded, I got a great jump out of the blocks. I stayed low in my best sprinter's form. In those nanoseconds, I felt like maybe I belonged with the big dogs until I realized that the runner next to me was already noticeably in front of me. I had to reach for another gear, and I did. Instantly, I felt a sharp pain in my left hamstring and I limped to a stop. Damn, it hurt.

I walked on the infield and Coach Whitey came over. He didn't seem very upset. "Keith, how in the world do you pull a hamstring within thirty minutes of running a competitive hundred?" he asked.

"I have no idea, Coach," I said. "I thought I'd stretched enough before the second race."

Looking at the back of my left thigh, Coach Whitey said, "Keith, we got a problem. Normally, you can localize the area of the hamstring injury by discoloration. With you, my boy, we better look for a different method." He smiled-even I thought it was funny. (By the way, Mr. Toothpick who I pulled a muscle trying to catch finished second. You know, he might have finished third if I hadn't pulled the muscle. Against much evidence to the contrary, that was going to be my contention going forward).

As the hamstring slowly healed, the FHS Demons participated in a couple of meets in which the team was only mediocre. In my absence, nobody stepped up and won events, even though we were competing against weak competition. The one team member who could have been a star was my friend Stan Detrich, who had been a consistent winner in the mile.

Tragically, just prior to the end of my junior year, Stan had drowned in a ditch designed to flow excessive water off FSU's campus. At the time, the creek had swollen as a result of relentless rain and had a rapidly-moving current. Why Stan, a genius in my view, had been close enough to the ditch to fall in would always puzzle me. But Mahlon and I already missed him. I'll never forget

Stan going to a Black house party with me and asking a Black girl to dance-she danced with him and he had done his best. That was in 1965, a year of volatile race relations but Stan didn't care. I admired Stan. He, like Tim, was just a decent person who didn't prejudge on the basis of color.

Mahlon and I were invited to his wake at one of Tallahassee's oldest funeral homes. As we walked in, we drew a lot of attention; in 1965, funeral homes were as segregated as movie theaters. I could not have cared less about the attention we received. We paid our respects to our friend and then left without a dry eye between us.

As we prepared for the state meet in Gainesville, I was feeling close to 100%. While I had not run a competitive race since my ill-fated hundred, I had worked hard enough to be in reasonably good shape to run the open quarter-mile, but I had serious doubts about my conditioning to run another quarter in the sprint relay at the end of the meet.

As I prepared to get out of the blocks, the one competitor that caught my attention was a slender 6'6" White guy, who I found out had won the hundred earlier. I tried to buoy my confidence by telling myself that no giant White guy could beat me in my race; I was wrong. The big guy nipped me at the end and won with a time much higher than my winning time the year before.

Oh well, I told myself, second place at state was no crime-although I felt like a loser given my "Number 1" status the previous year. By the way, the sprint medley I anchored came in third; and I finished third in the high jump at the supreme height of-you guessed it-5'8". (Inexplicably, I jumped 6'0 in a conference meet earlier that year.)

After my junior year, my dad once again invested in my future. He enrolled me in an intense 6-week mathematics workshop. All attendees came from different parts of the country (I was the only attendee from Tallahassee), and stayed in the dormitories on Florida A&M's campus.

The previous summer, I had gone to a 6-week biology workshop in Greensboro, NC on the campus of Bennett College, the college my sister attended as a rising senior. Both workshops were for exceptional students and were integrated (approximately 70% Black and 30% White). However, I'd be lying if I didn't admit that the most outstanding feature of both workshops to me was their co-ed status.

The workshops were my dad's idea-part of his on-going effort to have me reach my intellectual potential. Given that I didn't particularly like math or biology (although I had done extremely well on related courses and standardized tests), I had to admire him for his insistence that I acquire the academic background to compete with anybody. In contrast, even with its absence of girls, I almost would have preferred to go to a two-week basketball camp at Duke University-almost. (Mike Rhaney had gone and had come back considerably better in all areas of his game.)

I found that my game-as far as the ladies were concerned-needed its own workshop for me to rise to the level of mediocrity. This was especially true at the North Carolina workshop where I, as a rising junior, was a year younger than the other attendees. It seemed that the girls I tried to talk to were so much more mature than me. I was popular as everybody's younger brother, and I was told by many that I reminded them of Bill Cosby. I felt flattered by the comparison and, undoubtedly, overdid my efforts at being funny.

One incident at Bennett reflects my naïveté in the interesting dynamics of boy-girl relations. I had the distinction of being chosen out of the 20 or so boys in the workshop to take the college president's granddaughter, who was visiting for the weekend, to the on-campus movie. Since the president's home was almost in the middle of the small campus, the walk to the movie was considerably less than two city blocks. I found that I'd been chosen to squire the granddaughter around the campus because the president knew and liked my sister, Beverly, and because she knew that my dad was a top administrator at FAMU. As a result, it was presumed that I had good genes and knew how to be a gentleman.

Anyway, the granddaughter turned out to me absolutely gorgeous. She was about 4 inches shorter than me, slender with an angelic face, long flowing reddish-brown hair and a light-brown complexion. She was dressed "preppy" like me and when she spoke to me she was gracious, sweet, smart and sophisticated. I couldn't believe it, she was everything I wanted in a girlfriend.

I could barely watch the movie-a tired western-for looking over at her profile. We walked back to her grandmother' house, talking animatedly. I told her about my experiences integrating Florida High and she seemed impressed. She told me about her prep school in New Hampshire and I was definitely impressed.

When we got back to the house, the porch light was on.

"Would you like to sit on the porch swing?" she asked.

"Yeah, I'd like that," I quickly responded, almost before she'd completed the question.

We sat on the swing as it swayed back and forth. The sweet smell of honeysuckle imbued the moment with an idyllic ambience. I almost wanted to pinch myself. It was hard to believe that at 16 I had found my angelic soulmate. But next to me she sat.

I saw that something had fallen from above us and had landed on her arm. My angel jumped up, absolute terror in her eyes and screamed, "Godamn, motherfucker!" She started spinning around brushing herself off as she repeated, "What the fuck was that?"

I could hardly respond, the noise was too great of her falling off the high pedestal I had placed her on in my mind.

"It was a little chip of paint," I said. I picked up off the floor a less than two-inch old paint that had been dislodged by our swinging.

She said, "That scared the shit out of me."

I was, for once, speechless.

"I've got to calm down," she said as she opened her purse and pulled out a pack of cigarettes and a gold-plated lighter. In an awkward silence, she sat back on the swing and smoked her cigarette to the filter.

As I sat there and watched her smoke, I felt like she had cheated me of my image that she was the classic "good girl." She certainly was not the "perfect" girl for me as I'd thought. I knew of no girls who cursed like she had, and not that many boys.

I looked at her as she finished her cigarette; for the first time I noticed how heavily made up she was. She was not sweet, she was not classy; and she definitely was not the girl for me. (I conveniently ignored that she had never been my girl except in my lame, middle-class, Presbyterian mind.)

Somewhat abruptly, I said that I had to get going. I walked her to the door which she unlocked and stepped inside. She didn't look back and I said nothing.

As I walked to the dormitory I was met at its entrance by my roommate, a Black guy from Dothan, Alabama.

"Roomie, you are a bad brother," he said. "I saw you with that high-stepper at the movies. Talk to me."

I walked past him. "Not much to tell, really."

He followed me still pestering me about the "high-stepper." As I walked ahead of him, I could not get an old saying out of my mind: All that glitters ain't gold. I had found out exactly what that meant.

The workshop at FAMU the next summer was largely uneventful for the first four weeks. The last two weeks were memorable because I had a girlfriend-a girlfriend from Minnesota who happened to be White. Given my prior three years at Florida High, the whole White girlfriend thing was weird. But there I was, walking across campus with her, eating meals in the cafeteria with her and visiting her in the lobby of her dormitory. And people noticed.

My mother, who was in a day or two going to Tennessee in fulfillment of her Head Start responsibilities during the last week of the workshop, questioned me when I came home to get some clean clothes.

"Keith, I heard from a couple of people about you walking all over campus with a White girl," she said. "What? There aren't any Black girls around?" She had a bemused look on her face.

"Well, Mom, you know Bennetta dumped me and another one wasn't interested in me because she had a college boyfriend," I replied. "What's a guy supposed to do?"

So the last week of the workshop, my mother was out of town as was my dad who was running an educational workshop in Wisconsin. (Notably, I got my first and only "the birds and the bees" lecture by mail from Dad while he was in Wisconsin. Even way up there, he'd apparently heard about me and the White girl and, not taking any chances, had written a two-page, single-spaced treatise in his beautiful John Hancock penmanship formally advising me of the potential perils associated with involvement at such a young age with the female of the species.) I don't know if it was the absence of my parents or what, but for some reason me and my two-week girlfriend were 15 minutes late for curfew on the last night of the workshop. The people who ran the program went ballistic even though we were not the only students who had missed curfew during the workshop.

I was told that I was going to be suspended that very night from the workshop and would not receive a participation certificate.

I called home and told my sister, Beverly, who was twenty years old what was going on. She immediately told me she was on her way to the boys' dorm. She arrived some ten minutes later just as the two top administrators of the workshop called me to an outer office. Beverly walked in just as the workshop's coordinator was telling me that I had to go home that night.

Beverly stepped directly in front of me. "My name is Beverly Neyland and Keith is my younger brother. Starring daggers at the two administrators, Beverly continued. "Our parents are both out of town, but you probably already know that. So, I speak for my brother. You have no right to kick him out of the program if you haven't suspended every student who has been late for curfew and I know for a fact that you haven't (Beverly had to have been bluffing on this since, though true, I'd never told her as much). It seems that you're treating Keith differently solely because he missed curfew while with a White girl. I guarantee our father, the Dean of Arts and Sciences will sue you and shut this workshop down forever if you suspend Keith tonight."

I stood behind my twenty-year-old, 5'3" sister as she continued to stare the administrators down. I probably should have told them about Beverly. She has always been highly opinionated, serious, and the next time she backs down during a verbal altercation will be the first time. There's a reason that my cousin Charles and I called her "Miss Ann" starting when she was twelve years old. She was never a silly kid.

Beverly seemed to be the most authoritative person in the room, The administrators walked out and went to the middle of the hallway where they caucused. Upon their return, the top guy said only, "He can stay."

Beverly and I walked out of the office. I looked over at my older sister and almost started to cry. She had come and fought for her young, dumb brother. She was my hero; and she hadn't even threatened to sue their pants off.

1967-68
SENIOR

During the August before my senior year, I was introduced to the perils of Spring football. It encompassed incredibly long, hot practices; leg cramps that made you feel like you had painfully pulsating rocks in your calves; and minimal water breaks. But my perspective was totally different; I was a senior, the game was no longer foreign to me, and I was no longer timid.

It didn't hurt in the improvement of my comfort level that two other Black guys had joined the team. One, Bert, a sophomore, who had come to FHS as a 9th grader was a good-sized linebacker-type. The other brother was a senior transfer from Lincoln High. Terry Thomas packed about 225 on a 5'8" frame and having been a two-year starter at Lincoln, he was already a solid football player who proved to have very good athleticism and something of a mean streak on the field.

Off the field, Terry seemed obsessed with White folks liking him. Toward that end, he always tried to entertain any White students around him and I thought it was sad that in getting the White kids to laugh, he didn't realize that way more often than not, they were laughing at him not with him. While Ray Charles could have seen that Terry was being made fun of, Terry felt like being the Black jester was the way for him to assimilate.

In contrast to what I perceived my fellow students thought of Terry, a scenario in a Civics class, perhaps, indicated what many of them thought of me. During a discussion in class on the growing Civil Rights movement , the class got off on a tangent talking about race relations, particularly how historical mistreatment by Whites had resulted in many Blacks feeling inferior. A White student in the back good naturedly asked, "Terry, do you feel inferior to Whites?" Before Terry could respond, another student said, "Why don't you ask Keith that question?" Another student quickly interjected, "Are you kidding me? He thinks he is superior." The class, including me, laughed.

As I thought about that Civics class, I recalled that when Mahlon and I first integrated FHS, I really knew very little about White people except that they had virtually everything better than Black folks. They had nice restaurants, movie theaters, bathrooms at gas stations separately designated to accommodate men and women, better hospital and school facilities, the right to sit anywhere they wanted on busses, and they comprised almost all the actors on every TV show.

In comparison, I saw that in the Black community we largely had only what White folks permitted us to have; our material world was objectively inferior to theirs although, in my view, our love of God and of family was, at minimum, equal to (if not greater than) theirs. Under such circumstances, it is not a stretch to conclude that in the minds of impressionable Black adults and children, there may have been a latent sense of inferiority.

Fortunately, my dad was instrumental in a proactive way in telling me that the reason for the discrepancy in the Black and White communities had significantly more to do with the withholding of opportunities and other strictly-enforced oppressive measures than any inherent superiority of Whites over Blacks. Dad had the ability to maintain his dignity and to have his children do the same in the face of incredible racial degradation. For example, at many gas stations in the South there would be three restrooms designated for Men, Women and Colored. We suspended our bathroom needs as best we could on long road trips through the South so that we only minimally had to use the poorly maintained Colored restrooms. Dad was constantly reassuring us that the ignorance and intolerance upon which the oppressive Jim Crow laws were founded reflected the moral shortcomings of the majority rather than any inherent inferiority of Black people.

If I had any doubts on whether Black folk were inherently inferior to Whites, they were dispelled when, per integration, I got to see Whites up close and personal. I got to compare myself academically, from a standpoint of personal hygiene, from observed personal interactions, from manifestations of class (or lack thereof), and from evident adherence to Christian values. What I saw at FHS convinced me that the quality of White folk on various levels was hardly different from a similar evaluation of Black folks. No better. I realized that, absent integration, it may have taken me longer to come totally to grips with that singular truth.

I finally got assigned a full-time position at Flanker-a hybrid position which combined running and receiving. As the fastest, most elusive offensive player, I was dominant. Sometimes, I would purposely reach and catch passes with one hand or, after beating the secondary and catching long passes, I'd unnecessarily run all the way to the end zone. I found that in the open field when confronted by a tackler, I could throw instinctive moves that got me past the tackler frequently without being touched. And somehow, I knew how to run inside the tackles by setting up blocking angles for my blockers and quickly hitting the holes created by the angles.

During the Spring game which served as culmination of Spring football, I got the chance to test my skillset under game conditions. I was assigned to play tailback and took advantage of the extra carries to the extent I ran for just under 200 yards through the middle of the line and on sweeps around the ends. My self-confidence soared and I looked forward to resuming practice at the start of my senior school year.

Two significant things happened during the start of Spring football. The first involved a 1961 Rambler, an incredibly unattractive car (with the design of a small tank) that was parked in our driveway when I got home from my second Spring practice. I wondered, as Dad and I walked into the house, who was visiting. To my surprise, my dad said he had acquired the car for me to "use."

Though he acknowledged buying the car, he refused to say he'd bought it for me. No matter, for all intents and purposes, I knew it was my car. I ran out of the house with keys in hand and took an appreciative gaze upon the car. That same tired, white car that had been such an eyesore when I saw it in the driveway now looked to me like a sleek Jaguar.

The other more memorable occurrence took place on a weekend after the second week of Spring practice. I had walked to Jake Gaither Park with our beautiful collie, Bonnie, just to have a reason to get out of the house. (The park was so close to my house that my Dad used to stand on our porch and whistle when he wanted me to come home right then and there. My buddies would all break out laughing upon hearing the whistle because they knew I was leaving immediately, even if we were in the middle of a game of marbles.)

That day, I was tossing a tennis ball for Bonnie to retrieve when I saw a girl in pink pants bicycling toward me on the road that bordered the field where Bonnie and I played. I didn't at first recognize who it was until she got a little closer. It was Carol Awkard, and she looked great. I ran to the road and called, "Carol!" She stopped her bike and looked over at me.

"Hey, Keith. How are you doing?"

She seemed so calm and collected. I certainly wasn't. She was incredibly beautiful and I was nervous.

"I know your house is about a quarter of a mile down the street," I said, "but until today, I've never seen you in the neighborhood."

"I know, Keith," she said. "I almost never leave my house; I've allowed myself to live in isolation. But today I decided to do something about it-if nothing more than ride my bicycle to the park and back."

"Well, I'm glad you did. I haven't seen you since I played basketball at your school except for those few moments at Eric's party."

"Don't remind me. I'm still trying to live that down," she replied. (At Eric's party, Carol, who almost nobody knew that well, had rushed in and turned the table lights on to brighten a dark room that surely must have looked like a den of iniquity to any protective father of a daughter. Carol's father, who was known to be super strict with his three beautiful daughters, had seen the ruse because he had come in to check the environment of the party. He went over and whispered in Carol's ear and turned and walked out. Wiping tears from her eyes, she got up and followed her father out. There was much snickering, but not from me. I had really wanted her to stay.)

"I remember you playing basketball at my school and a lot of the nasty little things they yelled at you," Carol said. "I was mad at those paddies that yelled at you, but I was proud of how well you played."

Did she say she was proud of me? Beaming, I said, "It was nice seeing you with your schoolmates and I was so busy focusing on you, my coach started fussing at me."

She actually blushed. She blushed. I could not believe how sweet she was. We talked about 15 minutes before she said she had to go home or her dad would come looking for her. I didn't want her to leave. And before I knew it, I asked, "May I have your phone number?"

Realizing that we had no access to pen or paper, she told me to look up her number in the phone book since her family was the only Awkard listed. As she turned around and started to pedal away, she looked over her shoulder and said, "I hope to hear from you. See you later."

Bonnie jumped with her two paws on me and the tennis ball in her mouth. "Sorry, Bonnie, I just talked to an angel."

As Bonnie and I walked home, I thought back. This angel was out-of-this-world beautiful, she hadn't cursed once, wore no make-up and did not pull out a cigarette. I thought about what I'd learned from the girl at Bennett College. And smiled as I thought, "Some things that don't glitter can turn out to be (better than) gold."

The start of my senior year brought about an almost unthinkable occurrence. Along with Terry, Mahlon and I there was a new addition to our senior class-a girl named Bennetta. That's right. My former girlfriend who had unceremoniously dropped me for a "pretty boy" from Pensacola had for some unknown reason transferred to FHS from Leon High. Her transfer to FHS was even more bewildering because she would have no Black female schoolmates in her senior class.

On her second day, right after lunch, she beckoned me to sit with her on a bench just outside the lunchroom. "Keith, you know Rico-that boy from Pensacola, who I used to go with-and I have broken up."

"Yeah, I've heard about that." I had heard that she received phone calls from two girls claiming to be Rico's girlfriend. One of whom had threatened to come to Tallahassee and kick her butt if she continued the relationship.

"Anyway, I know you and I broke up and everything, but we had gone together for almost a year. I was…"

I interrupted her. "We didn't 'breakup,' you dumped me. Everybody in Jack N' Jill knew about it and I'm sure they laughed at me behind my back."

Bennetta's eyes were welling up. "Keith, all I can say is I'm sorry. But I went through the trouble of transferring here so that you and I can get back together. That's what I want. Don't you still like me?"

I couldn't believe this was happening; I'd had no clue. "Yes, I still like you; but I'm going with someone else. You should have asked me before going through all that trouble to transfer over here"

Bennetta was not expecting to hear this, "Not that ugly White girl from Missouri that I heard you were running around FAMU's campus with."

"She was from Minnesota, and she wasn't that ugly."

Relentless, Bennetta continued. "I hope you're not talking about Gayna, she said she wouldn't touch you with a ten-foot pole."

"No, it's not Gayna. But it is someone else."

She stood up and smoothed her dress with her hands and stood just in front of me. Undeniably, she was very good looking and she knew it. "Okay, Keith we'll see what happens." She turned and slowly walked away.

Looking at her as she sashayed in front of me, I felt my resolve weakening. She would be a great-looking girlfriend. I made myself stop watching Bennetta walk away. I already had a girlfriend; Bennetta could not make the call concerning whether she and I got back together. After all, she'd not consulted me to see if it were okay to dump me for Mr. Pensacola.

Since I spoke to her in the park, I'd talked on the phone with Carol virtually every night. It was so easy to talk to her. After a couple of weeks, I walked around the bend in Tanner Drive in our housing division to visit her. Her house which had a pool was the nicest in the division.

On my first visit, I was petrified with being confronted by her notoriously strict father, although he had given permission for my visit. (I always wondered if it may have helped my cause that my dad, the Dean of Arts and Sciences, was the direct boss of her father, the Chairman of the Psychology Department.) When he answered the door, he was all smiles and quite welcoming. He invited me into their family room where we sat down in a brief period of silence before

Carol walked in all sweetness and light. I was so happy to see her and enjoyed her company that night despite the fact that we were in her father's company the whole time. During my first visit I was also introduced to her mother, a Filipino lady who spoke in short, gruff utterances of heavily accented English that took some getting used to especially since she threw smiles around like manhole covers. Carol assured me that her mother was not as mean as she may have appeared. Early on,. in my mind, I had concluded that the jury was still out on that issue.

I later met Carol's two sisters, Jane and Linda, two drop-dead beautiful young women. Both Jane, a 21 year-old junior at Florida State University and Linda, a 19-year old sophomore at FSU were very cordial to me and seemed pleased that their baby sister had such an ardent admirer. After my first visit, I'm sure everyone in the Awkard household became used to me because they started seeing me at their home with the regularity of a bad dream.

So starting my senior year, I was in a good place; I was set for football season, I was a student with high academic standing, I was writing a column every two weeks for the school newspaper, and I had the girlfriend of my dreams. Life was good. My day-to-day school life for the first time caused me absolutely no angst. As a senior, I knew the ropes. I confronted no racial harassment at school and I was confident that I could take care of myself.

That's not to say that FHS became a bastion of racial tolerance. A handful of Black students were enrolled in 9th and 10th grade and, depending on their size, they were vulnerable to racial bullying. On one occasion after a pep rally in the gym, as I was walking back to the locker room I saw a White junior of pretty good size run up behind a smaller Black ninth grader, grab the younger student by his neck, pull his head down and, rub and pat his head. It was classic bullying intended to demean and humiliate. As laid-back as I was, I lost it. I ran up behind the bully and, grabbing him by the back of his collar, I spun him around and pushed him forcefully (and loudly) into some lockers. I put my right hand at his neck (I didn't squeeze) and held him firmly against the locker. He put up no resistance. Looking him in his eyes, I told him, "Don't you ever touch my man here again, Do you understand?" With a reddening face, he nodded his head and said yes. His face reflected his fear of the Black boy holding him by his neck.

I let him go and he quickly scurried away. The Black ninth grader looked at me with an expression of gratitude on his face that could not be faked.

"Thank you", he said.

"Anytime, my man, anytime."

We went our separate ways; I'd never had a better day at FHS.

In our first football game against Green Cove Springs. I was expecting that I would dominate the game from the Flanker position. As it turned out, Green Cove Springs dominated me. On four unimaginative sweeps, I ran for 10 yards on an unimpressive 2.5 yards a carry average. I felt as though I had dampened the expectations of a lot of folks as well as myself. I started to have some self-doubt wondering whether I had I overrated my abilities.

The next game against Milborne Catholic did not provide a definitive answer. I carried the ball four times on sweeps right or left and gained an average of just under 5 yards a carry. I had done nothing special until what turned out to be my last carry of the game. On that play, I accepted the hand off, ran toward the tackle position and found no hole there; I then bounced outside and outran the defensive back to the goal line. It had only been an eight-yard run, but it buoyed my confidence. In any event, statistically after two games, I was hardly setting the world on fire.

But all of that was to change the following week with the Sneads game which was our third straight game at home. Having played all but 5 of the total offensive plays of the two previous games, I felt as ready to play as I ever had. So, I went into the Sneads game believing it would give me a chance to shine.

It did. Inexplicably, after Sneads, which received the opening kick off and had successfully run two plays totaling nine yards, Coach Rose yelled to me, "Keith get in there for Maynard." I rushed onto the field wondering why I was being sent in to play defense when I rarely practiced on that side of the ball. I crouched in the cornerback position. When the ball was snapped, I saw immediately that they were throwing a quick slant. I ran toward the intended receiver, got there at the same time as the ball and hit him squarely in the chest. In a bang-bang play, the ball hit the ground and the receiver crumbled to the turf. Though the FHS crowd cheered, I had mixed feelings when I realized that I had just laid out the one Black player on the

Sneads team. I was glad to see him get up, albeit stiffly. I brought the ensuing punt 40 yards before running out of bonds when two Sneads players were closing in on me on the sideline. I was not happy to see that I had run out on the Sneads side of the field. For a moment the players huddled around me effectively blocking my return to the field. One of them, who looked like he badly needed a shave, said," Why you run out of bounds, boy, you scared to take a hit.' For a split second I tried to think of something to say, but, thankfully, before I could, the referee had cleared a path for me to get back on the field.

On offense , the first play called was sweep. My responsibility was to block the middle linebacker as he slid down the line to tackle the ball carrier, and with his eyes focused on the ball carrier, he was not expecting the flanker to come at him so quickly. As a result, he was completely vulnerable, and I gave him a shoulder shot which staggered him. After hitting the middle linebacker., I kept running to try to throw another one on the same play. I then threw a cut block on a defensive back who may or may not have had the capability to tackle Tim who was finally pushed out of bounds by a Sneads player on the 17-yard line. Coach McConaghey yelled to me, "Don't hurt anybody out there, Keith." For a moment I felt like a tough guy but I knew I still had a ways to go to reach that status.

On a counter play, I started to the tackle hole in the line when I dipped in to quickly assess whether there was an opening there and, seeing none , I bounced to the outside. Since the defensive back had taken a few steps toward the line when I first dipped toward it, after I started running toward the side line it turned out to be a race in which he tried to tackle me before I got past him. That race wasn't close. I went up the sideline for a 17-yard touchdown .

On our next offensive series, I ran another counter in which I was confronted by their best defensive back in the open field. I ran towards him under control as he crouched into a perfect position to make the tackle. As I closed in, I made a quick step and slight pivot to my left.; he fully committed to tackling me as I was going to the left sideline. But I wasn't going to the left sideline, I planted my left foot and juked back to the right with no discernable loss of speed. The defensive back stumbled and almost fell down as I went on for a 50-yard touchdown. The game was a godsend for my confidence. I ran the ball 4 times (was there a pattern there) for 95yards and two touchdowns, I caught two passes for 30 yards, I blocked like a maniac and brought a punt back 40 yards. Although playing only a handful of plays on defense, I made two tackles and intercepted a pass.

My performance in the Sneads game had exceeded my expectations. Unfortunately, I had no expectation for the following morning. I woke up with an extremely painful instep, for which I needed crutches just to be painfully ambulatory. I recalled having a sharp pain across the instep during the game, but played through it without notice. That I had shown no sign of any injury during the game probably explained the surprised look on Coach Rose's face when I hobbled in during our regular Saturday post game meeting. He called me over and, looking squarely into my eye, said, "What in the world is wrong with you?"

When I told him the circumstances of my injury, all hint of a smile disappeared. In an even voice he said, "Keith you have got to learn the difference in an injury and just being hurt. Football players especially Demon football players play hurt all the time. It's about individual toughness. I want you to rehab the hell out of that foot. I will call FSU's head trainer Paul Zeron and you make sure you see him every day after class and then come out to practice and watch your teammates work to get better and I'll see if you're ready to play on Friday against Madison. Remember, Keith real football players play hurt. You have to toughen up." He turned and walked away. (Interestingly, my visits to the FSU training facilities amplified to me the fact that the FSU football team had not yet integrated.)

I must not have been a "real football player' because, despite several visits to the FSU trainer where I received ultra sound and other cutting edge treatments, my instep hurt too much for me to play against Madison.

I was ready to go the following week against Crystal River. My strained foot was good to go and I was eager to take up where I'd left off in the Sneads game. Once the game started, it seemed as if I might outdo my performance against Sneads. The first three times I carried the ball, I gained a total of 29 yards. On my next carry, I was handed the ball and hit the hole between two of their tackles, one of my teammates (I think it was Terry Thomas) demolished the middle linebacker, and I only had a Safety standing between me and the goal line. I instinctively started to spin away from the safety. In mid spin, I was solidly tackled by one of their players who had apparently not given up on the play. He drove the top of his helmet into my side and I went down like I had been shot. Lord, did that tackle hurt. Coach Rose saw me limp back to the huddle and he, nevertheless, sent in another play for me-this time it was a deep pass to me. I was somewhat amazed that Coach Rose had waited so long to call the deep pass given that the player they used to cover me wore the Number 76 and was a big lineman. When I took off running, I suddenly found that my injury, which was later diagnosed as a 'hip pointer', was too painful for me to run at even half speed.

As I limped to the side line, Coach Rose came over, "What's the problem now, Keith? When I told him about the injury to my side, he turned and headed back to the side line with a strange expression on his face. As he walked away, I wondered what he was thinking and concluded that the look on his face had been "disgust."

Well once again I was visiting FSU's training room. I developed a good rapport with the Head Trainer. We talked about various sports. He told me how he and his staff went to all of FAMU's games even though it seemed as if they were the only White people in the stands. He told me that he had been hearing "good things" about my football prowess. He then looked around the otherwise empty locker room and, "I know I shouldn't be telling you this, but the recruiting staff has you on their radar. They are looking for a Colored boy that not only can play, but one who can also qualify academically. I told them from what I could see you were a very nice boy. So expect to hear from an FSU recruiter soon. Hey! Start stretching better and you won't get as many nagging injuries."

One day I was in the training room by myself as I rubbed a little ultra sound device over my injured side. All of a sudden there was a line of young men-virtually all of them Black-heading through the training room to the football field. Except for the fact that they all had the same khaki uniforms, the "DOC" letters on the backs of their uniforms was the sole indication that they were convicts. As a state university, FSU had apparently kept its costs for the upkeep of its football stadium down by utilizing convict labor.

As I set there, the stream of convicts going through the training room had dwindled to one or two here and there. One of them saw me on a training table and veered in my direction. Looking over his shoulder every other second, he quickly said, "Change clothes with me man; change clothes with me." I initially didn't understand and seconds after he asked, he turned to get to the football field with his colleagues. I had to think about this. He had not made a tough guy demand but had asked to me to voluntarily put on his khaki outfit thereby freeing him to slip on my gym shorts and t-shirt. I understood his motivation was desperation, but how stupid did he think I was. It was like the chicken asking the pig to join in providing a ham and egg dinner.

So I didn't play in our next game against crosstown rival, Ricketts because of my injured hip pointer; and it was not a lock that I would play the away against Jasper the following Friday. I spent the week before the Jasper game in a kind of limbo: going to the training room getting treatment and spending time on the sideline at practice trying to seem engaged. Because I provided no value to the team injured, the coaches ignored me. Likewise, since I was not practicing and had missed a couple of games, my teammates seemed to look right through me. I understood how my coaches and teammates felt- since I was unable to participate, even I felt like I didn't belong to the Demon family as Coach Rose liked to call our team. I was surprised that I cared what they thought about me but strangely, I found that I did.

Despite the negativity associated with my inability to practice and play, there was a phenomenon that at minimum balanced the scale: Recruiting contacts. While I had been contacted first by Tennessee Tech for track my junior year, after the Sneads game I started getting letters from various colleges which, to a one, told of their interest in me playing on their football team. Duke, Furman, Vanderbilt, FSU and Brown along with a number of smaller colleges to one degree or another told me of their interest.

I learned later that Coach Rose had sent game tapes to various colleges for the purpose of getting his favorites, players who had been with him and the Demon family from junior varsity, opportunities for scholarships. While I was sure Coach Rose wasn't distributing game tapes with me in mine (he'd become noticeably indifferent toward me as my injury-plagued season progressed), I concluded that the tapes he was disseminating for his favorites were giving colleges the opportunity to see what I could do especially if they viewed tapes of the Sneads game. I heard that Coach Rose had sent a Sneads tape to a school up north on behalf of one of his favorites, a two-way tackle. That college turned out to be the

University of Pittsburgh and, based on that game tape they proceeded to recruit me a lot harder than the other colleges that contacted me. A lot harder. I started hearing from Pitt coaches on a weekly basis usually just reminding me of their on-going interest in me and advising me that I could benefit the success of its football program.

Brown University contacted me more than any school other than Pitt. It touted its Ivy League status and the advantages associated with an Ivy League education. In contrast, FSU's interest in me was barely lukewarm although it provided me with three tickets to a home game against North Carolina State. (My mom and dad went with me to the game where Dixie was played at its beginning with the crowd rising as one, except for the three of us.) I vowed that I would not consider a Southern college because I was tired of the racial harassment. With that in mind I turned down an invitation from Duke to visit its campus after our season ended. Tim had accepted Duke's invitation to visit its campus and told me that it was good I hadn't gone on the trip because the players who showed him around had made racist comments.

Our next game was an away game against Jasper. Although my side was still somewhat painful, I had recovered enough from my hip pointer so that, according to the FSU trainer, I could safely get in the game for a few plays. On game night, after we'd won the coin toss, Coach Rose barked at me, "Keith get in there and return this kick."

Surprised at my early utilization, I ran to the deep return position as I fastened my chin strap. I awaited the kick-of on the 10-yard line. I received the kick-off on the 15-yard line and took off. I ran up on one of teammates blocking a Jasper player to the right I motored around the left of the two and ran away from players approaching me from both sides. An 85-yard kick-off for a touchdown had Coach Rose smiling at me again. At half time the score was still 7-0. (We won 24-7).

By the middle of the following week during which we prepared for our next opponent Pensacola Catholic, I felt I was finally at 100%. I looked forward to playing a Sneads-type game. Tuesday night of that week during one of my daily calls to Carol, she seemed especially excited to talk to me, "Keith I have a little token for you that I want to give to you before you go to Pensacola." We agreed that the following day I would stop over to her house and we could talk on the front porch. When I got there Carol came out to the porch, she was beaming. She immediately said as if she'd practiced what she was going to say, "Football is a rough sport and you've had your share of injuries."

"You've noticed," I said smiling

"Yes I have," she said seriously. "I 'd like to give you something that can protect you, not only on the football field, but in all your endeavors day to day."

With that she handed me a little ring box. It contained a small medallion on a chain. "That's a St. Christopher medal," she said while watching me closely to get my reaction. "It will protect you from harm, even from the Catholics in Pensacola."

Fleetingly, I had to wonder how, and indeed why, a Catholic saint would deign to protect a Presbyterian. I was, nevertheless, overjoyed to receive the medal if for no other reason than it had come from Carol. I turned my back to her and she clicked the chain together allowing me to put my new medal down the front of my shirt. "I don't plan to ever take it off. "I told her sincerely. In a perfect world we would have hugged and kissed each other good night, but in the world we lived in with her strict, overly suspicious father, we merely told each other good night and I went home where I couldn't wait to educate my family about my new protector.

Fortified by the medal I wore under my uniform and having no pains, I was ready for a huge game. And during the first quarter, that's what I got. While we didn't score that quarter, I ran the ball effectively and caught a quick slant pass on which I would have scored except that one of their defensive backs had reached and brought me down from just behind me by clutching my ankle.

The next play Coach Rose called a 10-yard down and out pass to me. As I ran the play I was to abruptly stop and turn left. I'd run the play a dozen times in practice with no problems. But that night when I abruptly stopped and pivoted left. I felt a sharp pain in my right knee. The pain was not debilitating although I had a noticeable limp. I noticed for the first time as I limped the 15 yards to our huddle that unlike any football field I'd played on, this one was very sandy with patches of sand all over the place.

Despite my noticeable limp, on the next play my number was called on a running play up the middle. I accepted the ball and tried to hit the hole as fast as I could. I saw that I'd gotten through the defensive line and I instinctively threw a move on the approaching safety. Then my knee crumpled and the pain for a moment blocked out everything else in the world. I dropped to the ground like a sack of salt. I was carried off the field by Tim and Terry unable and unwilling to try to put any weight on the leg. They sat me down on the bench and our team doctor came over with a cursory look at my knee. He saw fit to say to me only that I was done for that game. I didn't think you needed a medical degree for that observation. As he walked away, he advised me to place ice on it. Tellingly, Coach Rose couldn't find the time (even though he and the coaching staff stayed at the same Pensacola motel overnight) to inquire as to my well-being.

That night, Terry, Bert and I stayed in a motel because Pensacola Catholic had no Black players with whom we could have spent the night. Our White teammates were dispersed to spend the night with the families of the Pensacola Catholic players. While Terry and Bert had to try to sleep as I moaned in pain all night, they were as supportive and empathetic as they could be. In contrast, not one of the coaches who were all staying at the same motel deemed it necessary to come see how I was doing, nor to bring me something like an aspirin to combat the excruciating pain in my knee.

There was one thing I did that night that I felt compelled to do. I took my St. Christopher's medal off. I had planned on wearing it intermittingly, but as for never taking it off, the Pensacola Catholic game had convinced me that even St. Christopher had his off days.

That was enough for me. I was done with football that year and knew I wouldn't be playing in the last game against Bay High out of Panama City. I really didn't care as much as I knew I should. Basketball was my favorite sport and, during subsequent days of contemplation, I realized that my biggest concern was that I would have to miss basketball season. I didn't get a definitive answer from the orthopedics doctor Dad and I visited on Tuesday of the next week. I felt that the doctor, who was curt and distant, was not too comfortable with me and dad. I believed that he had a problem with our ethnicity. I may have been right in this conclusion given that the vast majority of White doctors in Tallahassee in the mid-1960's did not treat Black patients; and those who did most often had separate waiting rooms and entrances. In any event, after manipulating my knee, he diagnosed that I had a strained or torn meniscus. When I asked whether I'd be able to play basketball that season, he said that rest and rehabilitation might allow it to heal and if that didn't work I would need an operation. I asked if I got the operation right then would I be assured of getting the chance to play basketball that season. He responded by telling me to rest and rehabilitate the knee and we would see in a couple weeks if the condition of the knee had improved.

Two weeks later, with the pain in my knee reduced to occasional discomfort, I received permission from the doctor to start practicing with the basketball team if I wore a knee brace at all times.. When I showed up at basketball practice, some on the team seemed to look at me as an interloper because if I played some of them were guaranteed to get fewer minutes of playing time. But Mahlon, Mike, Tim, and Coach Albertson seemed thrilled to have me on the team and they were the only ones I cared about what they thought.

I was esthetic. I was going to play on a team that, despite losing big Karl Weiss, was going to be good. I looked forward to playing in the backcourt with Mike whose game had improved unbelievably . I thought that with his all-around game including an accurate jump shot that he could create on his own and my ball handling, ability to drive and defense we would be better than the previous year.

Those were the thoughts going through my head as I stood ready to participate in my first drill-a figure eight. I'd run these dozens of times and it felt good to pass the ball and weave in with my teammates in perfect coordination. As I reached end of the court and pivoted off my right foot, it all ended. My right knee gave way and I collapsed in pain. As Coach Albertson ran toward me with concern deeply etched in his face, all I could think was my knee had given way in the first exercise of my first practice and I would not be playing my favorite sport my senior year.

My non-participation in basketball was infinitely more painful for me than it had been in football. I had been good in football but I had been a vital cog on my basketball team. But the basketball season was not called off because I couldn't play. They went on and played and were led by the classic guard-Mike Rhaney. It got to a point that I could not go to the games because they were too painful to watch.

My knee was operated on in early January 1968. The procedure was so painful that, even though I hated needles, I, at times, asked for morphine shots which were utilized by the hospital to combat the otherworldly pain attendant to knee operations. After the operation, I saw myself as a nobody as I limped around the school. This sense was compounded given how quickly and how well the basketball team played without me. I had had no idea how much my sense of self-worth was premised upon my status as an athletic star. One force that balanced the "woe-is-me" mentality that I was struggling with was Carol. She was a constant positive in my life. I got no extra points with her because I played sports. Indeed, having gone to none of my games, I sometimes thought she liked me in spite of my status as an athlete. So seeing and talking to Carol made me understand that I was special to her no matter that, in my perception, I was no longer special at FHS.

Something else during my trying times of non-participation kept my spirits up: the University of Pittsburgh's unwavering interest in offering me a football scholarship. Even after my serious knee operation that caused other colleges to take me off their list of scholarship candidates, Pitt didn't back off one iota. I continued to get letters from its coaches and on-going requests to visit them as a recruit. Pitt did have me checked out by two specialists in Tallahassee who independently concluded that my knee was healing well and that I should be good as ever.

After its receipt of my knee diagnoses, Pitt and I set up a date in February for me to make my recruiting visit. I had no idea what to expect as I boarded the plane from Tallahassee to Pittsburgh. The awe I would have otherwise felt making my first airplane trip was subordinated to the uncertainty I would be confronted with in Pittsburgh. To my relief, I learned that my fear based on that uncertainty was unfounded.

When I deplaned in Pittsburgh, I was met by Dave Hart, the head coach and his wife. They drove me from the airport to the Pitt campus while identifying interesting points in the city with particular note of the looming Cathedral of Learning on Pitt's campus, the tallest educational building in the world. They both stressed how good Pitt was academically and how I could position myself for attaining a graduate degree. I subsequently learned that coaches rarely talked with Black recruits about academics except in the context of what were the minimum test scores and GPA they needed to get and stay academically qualified. I learned also that it was highly unusual for Coach Hart to transport a recruit and no one had ever heard of his wife accompanying him when he did.

At Pitt, Coach Hart passed me off to two of his players-a wide receiver from Raleigh and a junior safety from Pittsburgh. They were both nice and seemed to me to have it all together. They took me to my dormitory, in one of the three "Towers" and got me situated in one its pie-shaped rooms. They told me that I would have a roommate during my recruiting stay at Pitt, a defensive end from Buffalo, named Hank who was running late. The safety, Brian, told me that he had two dates to accompany us to get something to eat while we waited for Hank to show up. When we got to the lobby of the dorm, there was one girl with her back to us, "That's one of them." Brian walked me over to her and she turned to face us. She was very good looking and I remember wondering if I could talk to her coherently if she were my date. Not to worry. The fox was Brian's date; my date showed up a minute after and while she was a nice person, I knew I'd have no problem speaking to her coherently. The meal Bryant took us to was not at a nice sit down restaurant ,but a kind of grubby hot dog shop where you stood at or near the counter and consumed your hot dog(s). Players chosen to be recruiting hosts were given enough money to take recruits to nice places to eat depending on how much money the host hoped to keep for himself...Brian had apparently decided to keep a substantial part of his recruiting budget. After our" meal" we walked the two blocks to the Towers, said goodbye to our dates, and went up to the room to meet Hank

Hank was a 6'5", 250 pound Black guy from Buffalo. His hair was conked (processed with lye to keep it straight and shiny), a hairstyle that I'd always associated with Black gangsters. But everything about Hank smacked of a big northern city-the fast way he talked, his air of supreme confidence and his clothes which were as far from preppy (like the preppy outfit I had on) as one could get. He turned out to be a good guy and we got along well as we went to the various meetings scheduled for us the next day. In these meetings we met a Provost of the university, some boosters, some of the players and just before dinner, a couple of Black alumni.

All of the boosters seemed to know a lot about me generally saying things like how my speed would help the team. Almost to a one they referenced that I was from Florida and the fact that I must be good since Pitt normally recruited regionally. The two Black alumni, both highly-degreed Pitt graduates, explained how Pitt had not embraced Black students in the past, but it was their understanding that literally hundreds were to be admitted this coming September under special programs.

Along with the Black alumni, and a couple of boosters, we went to dinner at the Park Schenley restaurant as nice a restaurant as I'd ever patronized. Told to order whatever I wanted, both Hank and I went for the surf and turf which provided me my first taste of lobster-incredible! The alumni and the boosters repeatedly sang the praises of Pitt and how we would benefit from a Pitt education. I was impressed with the overall experience at the Park Schenley.

After dinner, Brian took us to a dance given by a Black fraternity, at the student union. It was fun trying to blend in with the college kids, at least until some street boys came in cloaked in long coats and Fedoras . I could tell that the Pitt students' comfort level decreased as they warily watched the street boys. Shortly after they arrived, someone yelled, "He's got a gun." Brian, Hank and I headed for the door like the other Pitt students. Back in our room, Brian said that Pitt, an urban school adjacent to "the Hill", one of the biggest ghettos in town, was just learning how to secure the campus from the street boys. My experience with the street boys was the only negative memory I had of my Pitt recruiting trip.

Just prior to leaving for the airport the next day, I met with Coach Hart one-on-one. He began our meeting by telling me that Hank had liked me and had asked if he and I e could be roommates I responded that that was fine with me. He asked if I were ready to sign a letter of intent indicating my commitment to attend Pitt. Before I responded, I asked him to what the letter of intent committed Pitt to do. He responded that once I signed the papers I would receive a four year scholarship to Pitt, that it would honor if I got hurt on the trip back to Tallahassee. It didn't take me long to sign on the dotted line. I was thrilled to have earned the scholarship and I could tell Coach Hart was thrilled to have me as one of his newest Pitt Panthers.

Back in school the following Monday, I found that the fact that I was the only football player at FHS to receive a football scholarship to a major university chased away the dark clouds which had been hanging above my head over missing basketball season. I felt validated as an athlete.

And as fate would have it, Coach Albertson called me into his office and, after inquiring as to the condition of my knee, asked if I wanted to join the team for the Conference championship game. I agreed contingent on my doctor's opinion as to my knee's condition. The next morning my doctor upon examining my knee proclaimed it okay for basketball as long as I wore a brace.

So there I was in the Madison High School gym on the following Tuesday running layup drills with my team mates. I anticipated sitting on the bench the entire game because I assumed Coach Albertson allowed me on the team as a formality so that I could say I was on the basketball team my sophomore through my senior year. The game was a tight one going into the last 4 minutes with us being down by five. When our point guard fouled out, I heard Coach Albertson call my name, "Keith get in there for Clayton." I ran into the game with nerves jingling, I felt incredibly self-conscious. But I got into the flow of the game quickly and made a steal and a tip in. But that's where the good stuff ended. In the last three minutes I threw the ball away for an egregious turnover and missed a put back that was so easy Ray Charles could have hit nine out of ten. We lost by two. Coach Albertson told me later on that he'd decided to give me a letter (for my letter jacket) for my senior year. My basketball career had ended at FHS.

Of course there were other things happening in the last third of my senior year that were not sports related. Mainly concentration by me and most other seniors was on those standardized tests needed to get into a good college. In Florida, the Florida Statewide Test was considered by all Florida colleges in deciding whom to admit. Students considering colleges outside of the state of Florida had to take the SAT. Mahlon and I took both. While I did very well on the SAT, I blew the Florida Statewide test out of the water (Mahlon and I scored around the same thing). I did so well on the Florida test (one of the top scores in my class) I was notified that I was qualified for admission to all Florida colleges.

Pursuant to the SAT, I was accepted at every college to which I applied including Brown University, Johns Hopkins, Franklin & Marshall, and Wesleyan University in Connecticut. I was a first alternate to West Point as sponsored by one of my congressmen, although my chances of getting in increased, I thought, when an Assistant freshman basketball coach came and talked to me about playing freshman basketball at West Point for a fellow name Bobby Knight.

I asked Dad about going to Brown, an Ivy League school and the most prestigious college, to which I'd been accepted. While agreeing with me that Brown was indeed one of the best colleges in the country, he pointed out that my four years at Pitt would be totally free and that my attendance at Brown would cost him and me tens of thousands of dollars. He didn't say anything else, but he, undoubtedly, wanted me on my own to do the math. I did and concluded that Pitt was it. (Brown, by the way, was apparently incredulous that its offering me admission was not accepted and sent me a letter asking for the reasons I'd passed up a Brown education.).

I asked Carol to my senior prom. She said yes, and more notably, her father did too. I was so proud when I picked her up in my family's Ford and we had a great time. I was particularly happy to see many of my classmates looking at Carol and also at Mahlon's date Celeste because I knew they'd have to admit that Mahlon-the "Yellow One" and me, the "Black One"-had two of the best looking girls in the house.

Track my senior year would be my last participatory sport at FHS. My love of track was certainly subordinate to my love of basketball and football. I never embraced the pain associated with practicing to run the quarter, nor the pain involved in actually running a competitive quarter. But having successively been the State champ and runner-up in the quarter mile my sophomore and junior years, I could not deny my aptitude for the sport. So I joined the track team right after basketball ended, even though my heart was not fully in it. Compounding my lack of enthusiasm for track was the slight swelling of my knee that I experienced after a couple of days of practice. I continued to rehabilitate my knee while taking a short break from running. By the time I had eased myself back into the regimen involved in getting in shape for the quarter mile, I only had about a fourth of the season left to try to prepare for the State meet.

By the time I was situated in my starting blocks at the beginning of the open quarter at the State meet, I felt that I was in reasonably good shape. I had run a 52 flat in winning the quarter at the Conference meet, my only competitive race during track season up to that point. That result had me assigned to lane 6; that meant there were five other runners who had had times under 52. I knew I would have my hands full. I had heard that there was a Black guy from Tampa who regularly broke 50. I looked over to lane 1 where the race favorite was practicing his starts. He was silky smooth out of the blocks and seemed effortless in hitting his stride.

I had to stop looking at him because doing so was causing an erosion of my self-confidence. I tried, instead, to concentrate on how I'd run my race. I made myself think that with my record in the quarter at the State meet, some of my competitors, including the Tampa flash, were probably taking side looks at me. That thought made me stand a little taller. I could win this thing, I thought, all I had to do was come in first. Nothing more. I found myself smiling as I got into the blocks

When the race ended, I had good and bad memories. The good: I saw no one around me when I crossed the finish line. The bad: I came in second and the reason I didn't see any body finish when I did was because the runner who won with a 48.7 was so far ahead. When I caught my breath, I walked over to the winner and told him he'd run a great race; he smiled and said thanks. As I turned to walk over to Coach Whitey, I noted that I'd found something somewhat disturbing about the winner. It came to me that emblazoned across his shirt was "Tampa Catholic." I realized as I walked away that I was getting pretty tired of Catholics derailing my athletic career. I promised myself that I'd better be ready when Pitt played Notre Dame.

So my track career ended with me winning one first and two seconds in the open quarter in three years. I also came in third in the high jump clearing my familiar 5'8". My senior year no one else from FHS placed in any individual event. I also was a member of the mile relay team (I anchored) that came in third. For the second year in a row, I was our high scorer at State. I would have given up those accomplishments during my last two years of track to have played basketball my senior year. Missing basketball my senior year was a difficult reality I had to carry for years after high school.

Things were seriously coming to an end in my high school experience. Surprisingly, I had mixed emotions. While I couldn't wait to leave FHS and my personal history there filled with an all-consuming angst founded in racially degrading day-to-day episodes, I didn't know how I'd handle college life especially the football part given how little I'd actually played the game (I finished my senior year having run the ball only 26 times though my average yardage per carry was a highly respectable 8.9).

With a week or so left before the end of my matriculation at FHS, the Annual Awards Assembly was held. At this assembly, attended by the entire student body, students received formal recognition of their school accomplishments. I knew Mahlon and I were going to be honored because we were told the day before to wear suits for the assembly.

The first award given was the first annual Stan Dietrich Award. Mahlon, Tim (also attired in a suit, but you expected him to be so honored since he was number 1 in our class), and I sitting next to one another, stood up and comprised a three-person standing ovation overjoyed that our friend's legacy would annually be recognized through bestowal of the award. We knew Stan would be pleased. As expected, Tim received several awards including one which recognized him as the number 1 student in our class, a Danforth Foundation Award and a Certificate from the Board of Regents recognizing his academic excellence.

Then Mahlon's name was called, and he went up on stage. I was surprised to hear that he was honored because he had been accepted at the U.S. Air Force Academy. I looked at him with so much pride. I hadn't even known he was considering the Air Force Academy. While others applauded from their seats, I stood up, as a one-person ovation, and clapped for my friend. During my earlier years at FHS because of my almost pathological self-consciousness, I would have never done anything like stand up in an assembly and draw attention to myself. But I didn't care about the extent to which I drew attention to myself, I was so happy for Mahlon.

While we had never been super close friends, Mahlon and I had forged a bond surviving FHS, especially the first couple of years, that transcended friendship. I remember our first year, we had to look out for each other, physically and, to some degree, emotionally. I recall that year that as much as I might have wanted to take an occasional sick day from FHS here or there, I knew that that was out of the question-I could not leave Mahlon to face that place alone. Mahlon for the same reason also had perfect attendance. We never talked about this because we didn't need to. We knew that as skinny ninth-graders, we needed each other to survive the on-going challenges.

Following Mahlon, a number of students received awards including "Citizen of the Year", a Civinette Scholarship and the "Daughter of the American Revolution." As time passed, I started wondering if some mistake had been made. Maybe I wasn't going to receive anything; they may have asked me to wear a suit because someone had confused the "Black One" and the "Yellow One" and had inadvertently asked me to wear a suit.

Sadly, that was my thought process when it was announced that the next would be the last award bestowed. Then my name was called. I walked on to the stage where I was met by a beaming Principal Bishop. Handing me a plaque, he announced to the assembly that I was the recipient of the "prestigious" Mode L. Stone Award, which was annually given to the student who best exemplified excellence in Scholarship, Athletics and Citizenship. I was familiar with the Award because from ninth grade on, I'd noticed that it went to guys who seemed to have it all together-in athletics, academics , and overall popularity. As I shook the principal's hand I thought about how I'd fit with prior Mode Stone recipients. While I had the academic and athletic criteria covered, my overall popularity was comparably lacking. As I turned and waved to the crowd, I thought that the folk who made the selection thought I was acceptable in each of the foundational criteria. I concluded that, under the circumstances, I didn't need to analyze my worthiness for the award. As I walked back to my seat, I remembered one of my dad's favorite sayings: "It's a poor dog that won't wag its own tail." My smile got broader. I concluded that the selection committee had made an excellent choice for the 1968 Mode Stone award and I held the plaque tighter.

The following week end the Jack and Jill Regional was held in Tampa. I had mixed emotions about attending because Carol had joined Jack and Jill a couple of months prior and would be on the bus with the rest of the Tallahassee contingent. Remembering how Bennetta had humiliated me at the last Regional by hooking up with

Mr. Pensacola and leaving me high and dry and disgraced in front of our peers, I was apprehensive that Carol, who was better looking than Bennetta, would be chased by her own pretty boy from Pensacola. But that didn't happen. The pretty boy was from Chattanooga. And he went after Carol when he first saw her in a seminar (I had gone to a different seminar). I was told by members of my chapter that he immediately sat in a seat next to Carol and talked non-stop. I was outside waiting when I saw him walk out with her. He and I locked eyes. He knew I was dating Carol; he had seen us numerous times at breakfast and lunch. As she headed my way, he suddenly turned and walked in another direction.

Seeing me watch the guy as he walked away, Carol said," He's been coming on strong, even though I've told him repeatedly that I have a boyfriend. "I realized that despite her incredible good looks, because she'd always been protected and isolated, she was surprised when guys hit on her. She stopped and looked me in the eye, "Don't worry Keith, I'm happy with the boyfriend I've got."
Throughout the Regional, Carol was with me even though Mr. Chattanooga and other Iranian looking brothers looked at her openly and longingly. I was so pleased that the lighter-complexioned and straighter-haired boys were made to realize that Carol's interest was in me-a Nubian. I was reassured.

Our graduation was celebrated the following Tuesday night. It was a beautiful ceremony with all graduates wearing beautiful burgundy robes. As we listened to the commencement speech by a young Florida senator, we were repeatedly told that the most critical thing confronting us as high school grads was how we chose to take on the future. For some reason the young senator's speech did not resonate with me. I strongly felt that the planning of my future would not begin with high school graduation; rather, I felt that I had begun serious evaluation of my future upon my admittance into FHS as a scared Black 9th grader. In my view, the uncertainty of my future as the first Black student at FHS in 1964 was equal, if not greater, than the uncertainty of a high school grad preparing to face college or other real world experiences. And as a 9th grader, I was less prepared to map out my future.

After the graduation ceremony, I hugged my beaming parents and Katrina and we had pictures taken of them huddled around me resplendent in my burgundy robe. I sought out Mahlon who was hugging his parents and Mike. I hugged Mrs. Rhaney and had an amusing flashback of her telling a White Mom complaining about the new "Colored" boys at the school that her son was Colored. I then hugged Dr. Rhaney, "Congratulations Keith, you guys not only survived over here, you actually thrived and I am so proud of the two of you especially dealing with that first tough year alone.

"Thank you, Dr.Rhaney."

Dr. Rhaney was a class act and I'd always thought of him as the best dad around after, of course, my own. Mahlon and I posed for a picture together arms draped on each other's shoulder. I really wanted that picture to compare with one of us taken shortly after we started FHS. I recalled that in the picture from 1964 we were not smiling and I remembered noting that in every picture we'd taken at FHS we were almost never smiling. But what had we had to be happy about. Yet here we were displaying all our teeth in a picture of us graduating from FHS. What a difference four years made. We'd grown.

I sought out Bennetta as she stood on the periphery of the milling crowd with her parents. I shook her mom and dad's hands and both were very cordial as they smiled warmly at me. I then hugged Bennetta. She and I had warmed up to each other after she was satisfied that I was with Carol and not going anywhere. Of course, she hadn't gone into seclusion. She knew she could get somebody else and she had a FAMU freshman who picked her up from school every day in a shiny, new Mustang. Without missing a beat, she had done better than me and my ugly Rambler.

I then looked for Terry. I found him going through the crowd spreading cheer as only Terry could. He was grinning ear-to-ear and bear-hugging graduates, parents and teachers-anyone who was remotely receptive. Upon seeing me, he put both arms around me and lifted me off the floor.

"How's my favorite Pitt Panther?

Struggling to breathe, I stammered, "Good, my man. I'm glad to be graduating from this place. And I'm glad you came over when you did."

Putting me down, Terry said, "I love it here. I wish I had another year."

I shook Terry's hand. "Well, give 'em hell as a Rattler," I said in recognition of his receipt of a partial football scholarship to

FAMU.

As I spoke to Terry, someone tapped me on my shoulder. I was shocked to see it was my classmate Buddy Paige the ultra-conservative who spoke of the Civil War as the War of Northern Aggression, of how much he believed in states' rights and of how the South would rise again. He was a true son of Dixie. But despite his good ole boy" ideology and admitted redneck persona, he had never said anything untoward to me nor did he hang with boys who went out of their way to demean their Black classmates.

"I want to wish you the best, Keith. I've learned a lot and really changed some of my thinking because I went to school with you and Mahlon."

"Thanks, Buddy. Best of luck to you." He turned on his heels and disappeared into the crowd

When I got home after graduation, and thought about the classmates and teachers I would in all likelihood never see again, I wasn't overly upset by that in the least. My year book had no entries in it. I was surprised, however, that I couldn't shake thinking about Terry. He seemed so happy when he was talking to White people trying to make them laugh-trying to get them to like and accept him. I thought it was sad.

In direct contrast, I knew that I had had little interest in assimilating into the White experience at FHS. I didn't want the White students or teachers to think that my overriding goals were to get them to like me and to emulate them. Rather, I strongly felt that I did not need White people's approval nor for that matter for them to like me to obtain validation of myself as a person. I was almost obsessive on this issue. In my mind, to go out of my way to be accepted by Whites made me an Uncle Tom, and this from a brother who dressed as White as the Whitest boy around.

My mentality in this regard is illustrated by my perception of a new Black female student who enrolled as a junior. She was a nice girl whose parents were both professors at FAMU. It seemed as if the minute she got to FHS, she sought out and joined those organization which interested her; and she became an active participant and leader in them. She seemed to have developed friendships with a number of White girls to the extent that she never hung with, nor ate with, other Black students. Shamefully, behind her back I and a number of my Black schoolmates referred to her as "Thomasina."

Later in a moment of clarity, I began thinking that objectively, she wasn't a Tom. Rather, she was an individual who refused to allow challenges in her educational environment to serve as an obstacle to her fulfillment of her potential growth as a leader or to inhibit her from making and seeking friendships that were based upon subjective standards other than race. In contrast, I refused to allow myself to remove impediments to my development of friendships, and to my efforts to reach my optimum potential as a leader. Rather, I chose to justify my lack of effort in broadening my horizons (relative to confident and ambitious participation in organizations, in defeating an almost crippling reluctance to speak up in classes for fear of saying something that was abundantly obvious or which made no sense, and in seeking out new and diverse friendships) to my not wanting to be an Uncle Tom. Maybe the real reason for my aloofness, however, was a subconscious fear that my efforts to become more entwined in the fabric of FHS culture would fail and I'd look like some pathetic Black guy trying his best to turn his back on his heritage and be White. I had to conclude that, at least in my situation, my failure to try to build friendships and to seek out avenues to the attainment of my fullest potential were not impeded so much by racism as by my voluntary use of race in dictating my behavior. I clearly understand that racism is disturbingly pervasive in our society and I recognize that it poses the biggest obstacle to the advancement of Black people.

I compared the behavioral traits of Terry and "the girl formerly and inappropriately known as Thomasina" and I saw that they were notably different-the former in dire need of elimination and the latter in need of emulation. I vowed to recognize the difference and to carry it forward in my life.

The next day, I went to FHS to clean out the last few things in my locker in the varsity locker room. I could have completed this small task earlier but, I think, deep down inside I wanted to come back and say my good by alone. Before I knew it, I found myself walking around reminiscing about what had become, for better or worse, my high school.

I walked down near the principal's office and looked at the long sidewalks from the student drop-off area which dissected the well-maintained lawn. I recalled that first day when I had mistakenly believed as we walked those sidewalks toward the great unknown that the students we would soon confront would be respectful and cordial to us as like Key Club members had been a couple of nights before. I turned and walked back to the lunchroom and peered inside. I remembered how Mahlon and I tried our best to be some of the first students there so that we could claim an empty table and not have to live through the degradation of sitting down to a table and watching the students get up and leave as if we were lepers. I looked down the long hallways and remembered how much I'd hated walking them from class to class and how, near the end of a class, I had to steel myself for that problematic walk.

My most poignant memory was triggered when I walked over behind the gym where Mahlon and I had retreated when we decided we'd had enough of the lunchroom drama. I looked at the spot on the back lawn behind the gym and remembered us choosing to eat whatever we could sneak out of our homes rather than the tasty lunches served in the lunchroom. I smiled, how pathetic were we. I had to thank God for Coach Albertson's intervention or who knows how long Mahlon's and my lunch menu would have continued to be Ritz crackers, peanut butter, Fig Newtons, boiled eggs and the like.

As I emptied the few contents of my locker and put them in a small gym bag, I retrieved a hair brush, a pair of old well-used sneakers and, I had to smile, from the very back of the locker, an almost empty bottle of Jergens lotion. Since my first day at Phys. Ed., I'd never had another surprise visit by the Ash Fairy since I'd always kept a bottle of Jergans in my locker. Walking out of the gym I stopped just before exiting and looked up at the track record board which recognized track records at FHS and listed those athletes who were State Champs. My eyes proudly lingered on my name as the 1966 440 champion and I noted that under the "records" part of the board, I was a member of the record-holding sprint relay team which occurred in Jacksonville in my first competitive race. Somehow my 5'8" high jumping feat was not acknowledged as it should not have been.

I walked out of the gym and headed toward the student parking area. I knew this was my last visit to the high school that had been such a large, sometimes all-consuming, part of my life for four years. Those four years were finally over; and I was determined to move forward to the next phase of my life. As I got close to the parking lot, I had an inclination to turn around and take a longing look at dear FHS. I ignored it and drove home.

That night, during a discussion of my high school experiences, Dad, out of nowhere, asked me what had been the most significant thing I could take from my high school years. After some thought, I begged off and told him to let me think about it and I would answer him the next day. In bed that night, I struggled with the question. After some analysis, an answer began to emerge. As I recalled my experiences, my mind kept coming back to Tim Garland. Starting with my first day in class as I was being targeted by the racist behemoths in the back row with a hail of spitballs, Tim had gotten up and walked over to the desk next to mine, sat down, and introduced himself. In my view, under the circumstances, what Tim had done was an incredible act of humanity and, for lack of a better word, fearlessness.

Our first couple of years, Tim and Stan Dietrich openly and regularly associated with me and Mahon. They did not have to do that; they could have been friendly to us without being high-profile about it. But they, and only a few others, chose to openly befriend us knowing that by doing so, they would likely face derision, ostracism, and vicious name-calling. I often wondered if I were in their shoes, would I exemplify the same courage. I hoped that I would have; but I didn't honestly know whether I would have been strong enough not to have taken the easy way out and been friendly with the Black boys, but not openly so.

Thinking about Tim and Stan, I formulated my answer to dad's question. Ultimately, the biggest lesson I learned from my high school years is not to paint with too broad a brush. In other words, I could never generally characterize Whites as being racist; non-empathetic or, otherwise, bad people. Certainly, deep down inside I knew that a race of people could not be all anything. (Black people were certainly not all good or all bad.) However, having seen the sacrifice made by Tim, Stan and a few others in associating with Mahlon and me, I viscerally understood that generally condemning any group of people as all having the same behavioral traits, provided a foundation for prejudice in its ugliest form.

With high school in my rear-view mirror, I looked ahead to leaving Tallahassee and going to Pittsburgh to become a college man and a football player-hopefully, in that order. My start at Pitt, however, was to be as a football player first given that the team was starting practice a week before students were due on campus with classes starting the next day. As a result, I had a nine-week period which I characterized as "purgatory" since it was between hell (my racially-charged existence in the racially-polarized South) and heaven (college life "up North" where I anticipated I would matriculate in an environment unencumbered by racial bigotry).

During that nine-week period, I worked out daily trying to strengthen my knee, gain some muscle weight and increase my speed. For the life of me, I could not gain enough weight to reach 175 pounds, but I could feel myself getting stronger, and, I felt, faster. The time I had which was not set aside for training, I was at Carol's house with the regularity of a paper delivery boy-every day. I was there so much I think I once saw her mother smile, but I'm not sure of that. Her sisters and her father were very accepting of my almost daily presence in their house and Linda her middle sister was kind enough to act as mandated chaperone so that Carol and I could go to the movies-the three of us. And to be fair, her mother turned out to be much kinder than her demeanor suggested (also she was an outstanding cook of soul and Filipino cuisines)

Carol and I talked with dread about my leaving for college and the related period of absence. Both of us agreed that our relationship would remain exclusive such that during the period we were apart, we would not date others. Recognizing that compliance with the exclusive agreement would be more difficult for me than for her because I would be on my own in an environment rife with coeds while she would still be under her father's strict control. For once, I didn't mind his strictness. We agreed to communicate with each other at minimum once a week by phone on Sundays in addition to letters during the week. When I had a week before I'd be heaven-bound, I showed Carol the blow-up of one of her pictures that I sent out to be enlarged. It was 3'x3' and she looked beautiful. I told her I was putting it up in my dormitory room. She seemed so impressed. I intended to do what I said. And, when I got there, I did.

I left the Tallahassee airport after saying goodbye to my dad, my mother, my sister, Katrina and Carol at the airport gate. Hugging everyone in the group, I received personal advice from each of my family members. Dad who is not a hugger by nature embraced me and whispered in my ear, "Study hard. Stay away from no-good people and when deciding whether to 'deal' with 'women up there', always remember what a great girlfriend you have here that you don't want to lose."

Mom, who is a hugger by nature, squeezed me tightly and said, "Eat a good breakfast every day and let me know if you're not getting enough to eat. Dress warmly and let me know if you need heavier clothes."

Katrina said, "When you call and speak to Mom and Dad, you'd better always speak to me or I'm coming to Pittsburgh and whip your butt. And I want you to bring me a Pitt sweatshirt or something when you come home for Christmas."

Carol, tears rolling down her cheeks, hugged me tightly. Just loud enough for me to hear, she said, "I'm going to miss you. I've gotten so used to seeing you almost every day." Through her tears, she smiled, "My family, even my mother, is going to miss you too."

I looked her in the eyes and said, "It's going to kill me not being able to see you. Just remember I'll be home before you know it. And we can stay in touch three to four times a week. We'll be all right. I'll be coming home for summer vacation in April. We'll be fine, just stay away from Pensacola and Chattanooga boys." She laughed.

I turned and started walking on the tarmac to the waiting plane. I looked back at Carol and waved. Having gotten so caught up with waving goodbye to her, I almost forgot my family was there too waving their hands like crazy, I waved to them and saw that my mother was wiping tears from her eyes.

I got on the plane and took a window seat. I looked out and saw my loved ones standing there waiting for the plane to leave. I knew that I had to make them proud. For a moment, I teared up. The love and support they showed me as I left that day was probably more than that received by many other young men my age who were in route to Vietnam where their lives would regularly be at risk. With that perspective, I even more fully realized how blessed I was.

Meeting with my new teammates was sobering. They exuded self-confidence and were huge and tough looking. It was hard to reconcile their look with a team having a 1-10 record the previous year, particularly with that single victory being a home game win against William and Mary largely, as the joke went, because William hadn't come.

While we initially met as one team, we soon split up with the freshman team going to a practice field next to the one used by the varsity. We did calisthenics and wind sprints and, while unspoken, guys were trying to impress coaches with their speed by finishing each wind sprint first. After a couple, I knew and they knew they were running for second. In the locker room after the first practice, I was approached by a number players asking one way or another if I was the wide receiver from Florida who was "supposed to be so good." Most were nice and welcomed me; a few, mostly defensive backs, sneeringly informed me that they would soon find out how good I was. As it turned out, I was good.

The next few days and for weeks afterward, I never practiced with the freshmen team. Instead, each day I ran pass patterns against the first team defensive backfield. I proved that I was capable of catching the ball, running crisp patterns, and getting open deep. Covering me turned out to be a challenge for the first team defensive backfield and any self-doubt about whether I was good enough to play at that level dissipated after a day or two.

With the first week of football over, I was ready and looking forward to students arriving and the start of the school year. I'd noticed that my team mates seemed to like one another especially those at the same positions. There were no racial problems whatsoever. The apparent harmony with which my team mates interacted underscored that my decision to leave the South for college was the right thing to do. That's why I was thrilled to be going to Pitt, a northern school where I envisioned a life finally free of racial animus. I was not going to college in an environment indelibly tainted with racial prejudice. I found it uplifting to know that I would not be inundated in college with the racial slurs directed at me especially how they had been during my Freshmen and sophomore years at FHS and at virtually all away games in football and basketball throughout my four high school years. I concluded that Pitt was different in a distinctly positive sense from any predominantly White, Southern college I could have attended. It had racial harmony despite a large influx of Black students through a program (Malcolm, Martin, and Marcus) implemented my first semester to affirmatively increase a very small population of Black students.

As I walked across campus to my dormitory in one of the three Towers" clustered together on the southern fringe of the college, I saw that the student body was multi-colored (White, Black, Brown and Yellow). It was enlightening to see that this world had many more ethnicities than just Black and White as my four years of high school had basically lead me to believe. In any event, I was esthetic to see that there would be many non-White students to carry the cross of integration and I would not be excessively called upon to support it myself.

When I finally reached Tower A in which my room was on the 18th floor, I stood at the area immediately in front of the two elevator doors with a number of other students. When one of the elevator doors opened, I and about a dozen other students crowded in. It was a tight fit, but everyone seemed to be in good spirits and there was a din of on-going conversations as everyone pushed the buttons for their floors. The 18th button was the highest of the nineteen floors in Tower A activated. Despite the fact that I'd be the last student on the elevator getting off on his floor, I looked around and saw that I was at the front of the group of all White faces and the only Black person on the elevator. No back of the bus for me, I thought to myself and smiled.

As the elevator doors closed, I gasped. Written at eye level in foot-high letters were the words I HATE NIGGERS. Since I was at the front of the group, I was stuck there with the offensive words seemingly inches from my face. I was transfixed and could not have looked away if I'd tried. All of the on-going conversations behind me ceased creating, in the small elevator, a loud silence. As the elevator moved upward, it stopped at six floors with students exiting on each. I moved to the side of the elevator to facilitate their exits. Though painful, I kept my head up and noticed none of the students made eye contact with me..

I experienced the same sense of humiliation I'd repeatedly felt at FHS. At each of the interim floors, after the elevator opened allowing students to exit, the elevator doors would close republishing the hateful words. This was wrong. I had not signed up for this. I felt betrayed, but I didn't know by whom. The elevator doors opened on Floor 17 and the last two students stepped out on their floor. Alone in the elevator, the offensive words seemed to be 10-feet tall and seemed like they were directed solely at me. I felt anger and humiliation in equal parts as I had so frequently felt ae FHS. I concluded that there was a void in my processing that episode and I had to think about what that void was. It finally occurred to me: Where was Mahlon when I needed him. It hit me that even though there were a number of non-White students on campus, I felt a void because I had come to rely on Mahlon and my dad to help me process direct acts of racism. As I thought it through, I knew, nevertheless, that henceforth I would learn to deal with racism as filtered through my own psyche.

As I walked out of the elevator, I realized the source of the "betrayal" which had engendered the pain I was feeling-my naiveté. I had simplistically concluded that I could run away from racism. the words on the elevator door underscored a basic premise: the universality of racism is such that while you can continually run from it, you can never hide from it.

As I walked into my dormitory room, I knew that I had, perhaps, attained a higher level of sophistication from the elevator scenario. While I would never be able to avoid racism and its negative impact, my goal was to control its impact on me. My four years at Florida State University High School taught me that I should not allow manifestations of racism to dehumanize me. Rather, I should look at the involved racist and realize that he or she had, in fact, dehumanized themselves. I came to realize that an ignorant racist should never make me feel bad about myself. I know it's going to be one of the on-going battles of my life; but I'm prepared for that battle. After all, I am a Nubian Warrior.

Made in the USA
Columbia, SC
07 December 2021

50656401R00090